Contemporary 21st Century Strategic Human Resources Management: A Biblical Perspective

by

Aaron B. Locklear, MBA, MSc.HRM

© **Copyright 2024 by** – Aaron B. Locklear. **All rights reserved.**

The following book is reproduced below to provide information that is as accurate and reliable as possible. Regardless, purchasing this book can be seen as consent that neither the publisher nor the author is an expert on the topics discussed and that any recommendations or suggestions made herein are for entertainment purposes only.

Professionals should be consulted as needed before undertaking any of the actions endorsed herein. This declaration is deemed fair and valid by the American Bar Association and the Committee of Publishers Association and legally binding throughout the United States.

Furthermore, the transmission, duplication, or reproduction of any of the following work, including specific information, will be considered illegal, whether done electronically or in print. This extends to creating a secondary, or tertiary copy of the work or a recorded document and is only allowed with express written consent from the publisher. All additional rights reserved.

The information in the following pages is broadly considered a truthful and accurate account of facts, and as such, any inattention, use, or misuse of the information in question by the reader will render any resulting actions solely under their purview. There are no scenarios in which the publisher or the author of this work can be deemed liable for any hardship or damages that may befall them after undertaking the information described herein.

Additionally, the information in the following pages is intended only for informational purposes and should thus be considered universal. As befitting its nature, it is presented without assurance regarding its prolonged validity or interim quality. The trademarks mentioned are made without written consent and cannot be considered an endorsement from the trademark holder.

Table of Contents

Acknowledgments..5

Personal HRM Consultative Experience & Practices in the 21st Century...8

Preface..12

Chapter 1: Introduction to Human Resource Management..................16

Chapter 2: Contemporary 21st Strategic Human Resources Management (SHRM) 36

Chapter 3: Leadership 51

Chapter 4: Organizational Strategy 65

Chapter 5: Performance Management..79

Chapter 6: Talent Management 92

Chapter 7: Mergers and Acquisitions (M&A) 106

Chapter 8: Learning and Development (L&D) 119

Chapter 9: Total Rewards..131

Chapter 10: Employee Relations..145

Chapter 11: Employee Engagement...159

Chapter 12: Diversity Management...172

Chapter 13: Employee Wellbeing, Work-Life-Balance, and Health..186

Chapter 14: Change Management..198

Chapter 15: Compliance & Risk Management.........................212

Chapter 16: Reasonable Accommodations................................225

Chapter 17: Religious Accommodations.....................................238

Chapter 18: HRIS and Advanced Technology Integration.......247

Part II: SHRM Applications in the Public Sector SHRM..........261

Chapter 19: U.S. Federal Government..266

Chapter 20: State Government...278

Chapter 21: Local and Municipal Governments.......................292

Chapter 22: PESTEL Framework..306

Chapter 23: SHRM Outlook & Trends in 2024 and beyond....321

Chapter 24: Epilogue..326

Glossary of Terms 332

Author Bio..440

Acknowledgments

The journey to complete this book "Contemporary Strategic Human Resources Management: A Biblical Perspective" has been filled with challenges, opportunities, and precious moments of insight. The publication of this work is a testament not only to my efforts but to the support, guidance, and inspirational insights of countless individuals who have been instrumental in molding this book. I extend my deepest gratitude to all who have been part of this journey.

Firstly, my profound thanks go to God the Father, Jesus Christ the Son, and the Holy Spirit, for the guidance, strength, and wisdom throughout this journey. This book is a testament to faithfulness—as it merges lessons from scripture with modern HR strategies, which undoubtedly, is a testament to God's divine inspiration.

My heartfelt thanks go to my family, who have been my constant source of support and encouragement throughout the writing process. Your unending faith in my abilities has been the force that propelled me onwards even in the face of obstacles.

I would also like to thank my esteemed colleagues from the field of Human Resource Management. Your vast knowledge and open-minded discussions have provided enriching insights into the contemporary trends in Strategic HRM.

My gratitude goes out to all those in the academic world whose work directly or indirectly inspired and guided this project. I have learned immensely from your rigor, dedication, and passion.

Lastly, I must express my profound gratitude to all the readers who put their faith in me and this book. My earnest hope is that the content within these pages will enlighten you, inspire you, and provide you with valuable insights that merge the timeless teachings of the Bible and the strategic elements of modern Human Resource Management.

To all I have mentioned thus far, and to the countless others who have been part of this journey, you have my respect and deepest appreciation. I thank you from the bottom of my heart for your lasting impact on me, personally and professionally, in the journey of creating this book.

God bless you all.

Personal Consultative Knowledge & Practices in 21st Century

As an HR expert in the increasingly complex and dynamic business world, my role leverages diversified experience and knowledge of human resource principles to explore and implement effective solutions around the key areas of HR. These areas include but are not limited to talent management, workforce planning, performance management, training and development, employee benefits, compensation, and employee relations.

The emphasis on strategic HRM is a response to the demanding nature of today's global business environment. Therefore, besides processing daily transactions and handling HR administrative tasks, my services consider overarching questions about how to manage and motivate people for better productivity, engagement, and satisfaction.

Talent management, for instance, involves not just hiring the right individuals but also fostering a supportive and inclusive company culture that embraces diversity, continuity, and mutual growth. Comprehensive onboarding programs, continuous professional development activities, career laddering, and succession planning are aspects I delve into.

I guide in constructing a balanced performance management system that goes beyond annual appraisals to include regular feedback, goal setting, employee recognition, and avenues for candid conversations between employees and their managers. Training and development tasks that I oversee include identifying skills gaps and deploying cost-effective, engaging learning solutions that cater to the preferences of the modern employee.

In terms of compensation and benefits, my focus is on maintaining market competitiveness while ensuring internal fairness among employees. I help businesses devise salary structures, benefits packages, and incentive schemes that satisfy employees' needs and incentivize high performance.

Lastly, employee relations are a crucial area where I can assist in building and maintaining a harmonious workplace. Whether resolving conflicts, addressing grievances, driving employee engagement activities, or ensuring legal compliance, my aim is to create a positive work environment conducive to high performance.

Overall, as an HR expert, I play a critical role in helping your organization achieve its strategic goals through people-centered strategies. I firmly believe that an organization's most valuable asset is its workforce - an asset that, with sound human resource practices, can deliver exceptional results.

Preface

In recent years, the field of strategic human resources management has undergone dramatic evolutions and transformative shifts. This book seeks to anchor these shifts within a novel frame of reference: a Biblical worldview. It is our conviction that while secular theories and practices of human resources management have their merits, the Biblical worldview provides a remarkably rich, diverse, and profound perspective on the subject.

The world of work is central to human life and, therefore, to the Biblical narrative. The Bible talks extensively about work and workplace relationships, offering invaluable insights on issues such as leadership, wisdom, ethics, justice, conflict resolution, and motivation. In framing these within a strategic human resources context, the book aims to provide a refreshing, innovative, and enriching discourse on the subject.

This book offers a Christian interpretation based on a Biblical worldview - incorporating principles and values presented in the Old and New Testaments. Drawing from experience and scholastic knowledge, as well as a multitude of Biblical passages, this book explores specific strategic human resources themes such as talent acquisition, workforce engagement, organizational culture, diversity and inclusion, and performance management. At the same time, it pioneers a systematic incorporation of Biblical values like stewardship, servanthood, love, integrity, and righteousness into these themes.

This book is intended for human resources practitioners, scholars, students, and other professionals interested in the intersections between strategic human resources management and spiritual perspectives. It will also be of particular interest to those involved in faith-based organizations who seek a more integrated approach to their work. It is our hope that readers will find this book a thought-provoking and illuminating exploration into uncharted territory in human resources and organizational management.

In this venture, we have intentionally sought balance, careful not to reduce Biblical texts into mere management tools, nor to impose religious beliefs on organizational practices. Instead, we have strived to offer a robust analytical, critical, and conceptual framework that respects the depth and richness of the Biblical text while remaining relevant to contemporary strategic human resources concerns.

In essence, this book embodies a deep appreciation of the human dimension of work, inspired by a Biblical worldview. This perspective sees employees as more than 'human resources' but as unique individuals with inherent dignity, created in the image of God, and entrusted with talents and gifts to be nurtured, developed, and deployed for the common good. This is the deeper, more holistic approach to strategic human resources management that this book seeks to foster.

The author aspires that this volume will provoke a robust dialogue, inspire further exploration, and contribute to the ongoing development of a more compassionate, equitable, and humane approach to strategic human resources management.

Chapter 1: Introduction to Human Resources Management

The evolution of Human Resources Management (HRM) has traveled a rich and diversified path since the Civil War era to current 21st-century strategic HRM practices. It has gone through a significant transformation, from a traditional administrative function to a strategic partner. The period following the Civil War in America was characterized by significant changes in multiple spheres of life, largely affected by the Industrial Revolution, which was operating in full force. Increased mechanization and the development of new technologies spurred drastic growth across numerous sectors.

The flourishing of factories, industries, and railroads reshaped the employment landscape, essentially cultivating new occupations and expanding job opportunities. As labor shortages were filled rapidly, an urgent need arose to effectively manage these workforces, leading to the emergence of roles analogous to the modern human resources (HR) function.

'Welfare secretaries' was one such position that evolved during this period. Rather than managing strategic human resources, their role was primarily transactional in nature, covering rudimentary aspects of what we know as HR today. Primarily, their task was to execute basic yet essential organizational responsibilities such as managing employees' payroll, ensuring they received appropriate rewards for their work, and attending to their safety and welfare concerns. Each of these responsibilities was, and still is, an essential component in maintaining a productive and motivated workforce.

The operation of these HR functions during this industrial season was significantly simplistic as compared to the complex models applied in contemporary HRM (Human Resource Management). The primary focus was on transactional activities including record keeping, wage management, hiring, and firing. The rationale for such simplicity can be attributed to the infancy of the HR function, apart from the less complex labor laws and industrial regulations that existed during the period.

Record-keeping was an indispensable duty, ensuring every employee's work history, achievements, and misconduct were adequately documented. The wage management function saw to it that all employees were compensated fairly and accurately for their work, an exercise that also factored in overtime payments where applicable.

Hiring and firing was another key task, which involved the recruitment of new employees and the dismissal of those whose services were no longer needed.

With the advent of Scientific Management in the early 20th century under the guidance of Frederick Winslow Taylor, the focus of business began to shift towards an emphasis on efficiency. A significant concept introduced during this era was the notion that workforce productivity was not only linked to their physical capabilities but also the under-utilized potential of their intellect. This heralded a new perspective, where the workforce was not just an assembly of manual labor but a pool of intellectual resources. Hence, the Human Resources (HR) focus transformed towards the appropriate selection, training, and development of employees.

The principles of Scientific Management coupled with a keen understanding of human behavior, lead to an optimal working environment, which in turn results in an increase in productivity and profitability. The concepts of job design, work simplification, and standardization began gaining relevance as companies aimed for higher efficiency and lower wastage.

Around this time, another vital development was the outcome of Elton Mayo's Hawthorne Studies which accentuated the importance of human relations in the workplace. The studies revealed that employees were not only driven by monetary gains but also by emotional needs such as acknowledgment and a sense of belonging. It was concluded that a happy and motivated workforce significantly outperforms a demotivated one, leading to the birth of the Human Relations movement. This movement triggered the formation of numerous employee welfare policies and motivational programs, which are still relevant and prevalent in modern HR functions. Health insurance and retirement plans started becoming commonplace, marking a significant departure from the conventional employment model. The focus was not just on recruitment and payroll anymore but extended to ensuring the financial and health security of employees in the long run, recognizing the importance of employee wellbeing, productivity, and consequently, their retention.

This wave presented the inception of 'Personnel Management', an employment paradigm shift that managed a wider range of responsibilities. The emphasis was not only on adhering to employment laws and managing labor relations but also defined as an organization's responsibility to appraise performance, motivate employees, and provide them with the necessary training and development to enhance their skills. Consequently, an improved and harmonious relationship between employers and employees was deemed essential, leading to the strengthening of employee relations at the workplace. The essence of Personnel Management was to maintain a just and equitable workplace environment where everyone was treated fairly and where the rights of both employer and employees were respected. Hence, it served as the foundational base for Human Resource Management as we know it today.

The late 20th century was marked by the rise of globalization and intense competition. HR professionals began to realize that their most significant corporate assets were their employees. This is where strategic HR management started to materialize, recognizing the importance of aligning HR activities with the organization's strategic goals.

With the arrival of the 21st Century, the focus has shifted more to strategic HRM. It involves proactive forecasting and management of manpower needs, developing and retaining top performers, succession planning, and integration with business strategy. Technology has emerged as a pivotal enabler in HR practices, with electronic HRM (e-HRM) and HR Information Systems (HRIS) helping the HR departments to become more efficient and to gain strategic insights into the workforce.

In the contemporary business landscape, the human resources department plays a multi-dimensional role. It is actively involved in aspects like human capital management (HCM), diversity management, domestic and/or international talent acquisition, corporate social responsibility, employer branding, and reputation management. The focus is not merely on manning the infrastructure but also on shaping the brand image and ensuring the strategic development of the company.

Diversity management is one of the crucial facets of HRM today. An inclusive work environment is not only ethically correct but also creatively enriching. A diverse workforce encourages the exchange of different perspectives, fostering innovation, and providing a broader range of solutions to problems. Moreover, a diverse and inclusive workforce is more representative of the global customer base, which in turn enhances customer relations and satisfaction.

In the contemporary globalized world, acquiring talent is no longer just confined to the local labor market. The hunt for the right talents has gone beyond borders, seeking individuals from every corner of the world. Advancements in technology have made global talent acquisition a possibility and HR departments actively participate in hunting, attracting, and retaining such a diverse and universal talent pool.

Employer branding and reputation management are other critical aspects of HRM that work towards creating a positive image of the company among potential employees and the public in general. An organization can attract top talent to their firm by projecting a positive company culture and attractive benefits and opportunities.

Corporate Social Responsibility (CSR) is another area where HR plays a significant role in implementing and promoting ethical practices within the organization. It helps in building a positive brand image and fosters trust among employees, customers, and stakeholders, to generate a long-term sustainable triple bottom line.

Finally, HRM is actively involved in the planned development of the organization. Aligning HR strategies with organizational strategies helps achieve the overall organizational mission, vision, and goals more effectively and efficiently. By managing organizational culture, facilitating change, and developing skills and capabilities among workers, Strategic HR ensures that the organization is on the right path to sustainability and success.

Today, HR has emerged as a strategic partner in the business community, playing a vital role in shaping and nurturing the organization's human assets. The broader implications of HRM cannot be overlooked and are instrumental in ensuring an organization's sustainability and strategic development.

Overall, the evolution of HRM from the Civil War era to the current 21st century is a journey riddled with transformations and innovations. Each era has left indelible imprints on HRM's evolutionary path, shaping it as a key driver of an organization's strategic progress. Today, while technology is indeed a game-changer, the human touch remains the cornerstone of good HR practices.

Transforming HRM from Traditional to Strategic at XYZ Corp: Case Study

Founded in 1995, XYZ Corporation is a leading supplier of industrial automation in the United States. Since its inception, it has been operating with a traditional Human Resource Management (HRM) approach, focusing mainly on the administrative side of HR, such as record-keeping, compliance, and HR operations.

Transformation to Strategic HRM:

In 2018, the HR Director at XYZ Corporation realized that managing human resources more strategically and coherently could contribute more to the growth of the organization and was crucial to its success. Thus, the transition from a traditional HR approach to a strategic one was initiated.

Strategic HRM Planning:

The HR department began an in-depth analysis of the company strategy and developed a comprehensive understanding of where XYZ Corporation wanted to be in the next five years. This served as a guide to re-orient the HR functions aimed at maximizing the potential of its human resources to achieve these strategic goals.

Staff Development and Performance Management:

The emphasis on training, as well as learning and development (L&D) programs, was increased. Rather than simply focusing on job-specific training, the new approach looked at the overall development of their employees and how their skills could align with the company's strategic goals. This was supplemented by a performance management system geared towards goal alignment, employee accountability, and continuous feedback.

Integration of HRM and Line Management:

XYZ Corporation also transformed its approach to line management. In the traditional HRM model, a clear divide existed between the HR department and line managers. Under the strategic model, this division was blurred, with HR professionals working closely with line managers to ensure that all decisions were in line with the overall strategic goals of the organization.

Employee Engagement:

The new HRM strategy adopted by XYZ Corporation placed significant emphasis on employee engagement. Recognizing that their employees were one of their biggest assets, XYZ Corporation worked on developing an organizational culture that fostered engagement, motivation, and satisfaction.

Results:

The transition from traditional HRM to strategic HRM at XYZ Corporation wasn't immediate; it required time, effort, and a cultural shift. However, the results were tangible and noteworthy. Employee productivity and engagement rose noticeably. Moreover, the strategic alignment between the HR department and the overall organizational goals contributed significantly to the implementation of strategic plans at XYZ Corporation.

Conclusion:

The transformation of HRM at XYZ Corporation from traditional to strategic has served as an influential model demonstrating how strategically oriented HR activities can contribute to an organization's success. It underlines the fact that HRM must not be confined to administrative tasks but should play a more central role in achieving an organization's strategic objectives.

Human Resources Management: A Biblical Perspective

The role of Human Resources (HR) is pivotal in every organization as it bridges the relationship between employees and employers, ensuring smooth business operations. HR management (HRM) can be enriched when viewed from a biblical worldview perspective, providing both ethical and moral guidance.

Firstly, it is important to recognize the dignity and worth of each employee, as stated in Genesis 1:27 (KJV) - "So God created man in his own image, in the image of God created he him; male and female created he them." This biblical principle is a reminder to treat everyone with respect and fairness regardless of their job role or ranking. Every individual brings unique value and talent to the organization.

Also, leadership is a significant aspect of successful HR management. Jesus himself is considered the perfect biblical model of leadership. In Mark 10:44 (KJV), Jesus taught His disciples about a new paradigm of leading by saying, "And whosoever of you will be the chiefest, shall be servant of all." This verse encourages servant leadership, where power and authority are used for the benefit of the employees rather than for personal gain.

The Bible also speaks to honesty, integrity, and transparency in dealings. Proverbs 11:3 (KJV) states, " The integrity of the upright shall guide them: but the perverseness of transgressors shall destroy them." HR policies and practices must reflect these virtues, fostering a trustful and secure work environment.

Labor relations is another area that the Bible addresses directly. Colossians 4:1 (KJV) states " Masters, give unto your servants that which is just and equal; knowing that ye also have a Master in heaven." This likewise applies to employer-employee relationships today. It emphasizes the importance of fair pay, reasonable work conditions, and respect for workers' rights.

Finally, the Bible encourages personal and professional development. Proverbs 22:29 (KJV) says, "Seest thou a man diligent in his business? he shall stand before kings; he shall not stand before mean men." This highlights the value of investing in personal growth and learning, which leads to success and recognition.

Adopting a biblical worldview perspective in HR management promotes an ethical, respectful, and productive work environment where everyone is treated fairly and given an equal opportunity to thrive. It further encourages moral leadership, transparency, the fair treatment of workers, and continual personal development. This approach can help HR management to navigate the many challenges they face while fostering a positive workforce and successful organization.

Chapter 2: Contemporary Strategic Human Resources Management (SHRM)

In the evolving business landscape of the 21st century, the role of strategic human resources management (HRM) has transformed from a traditional administrative function to a crucial driver of organizational effectiveness and sustainability. Contemporary strategic HRM is an integrative process that holds the potential to contribute substantially to the company's success.

1. **Strategic Planning**: At the helm of HR's strategic tasks is developing long-term workforce plans that align with the company's corporate strategy. This involves evaluating the current workforce, forecasting future HR needs, and devising strategies to bridge the gap.

2. **Talent Management**: HRM's role in talent management extends beyond hiring to the development and retention of high-quality employees. This embraces talent acquisition, onboarding, performance management, training and development, succession planning, and employee retention strategies.

3. **Performance Management**: In an era of increased competition and changing business goals, performance management has cemented its role as a key HRM function. Through regular performance reviews, MBOs, and 360-degree feedback, HR can ensure that employee's performance aligns with the organization's objectives.

4. **Total Reward Management**: Total Reward systems, both tangible (money) and intangible (recognition), are strategic tools in HRM. They

serve to motivate employees, enhance job satisfaction, reduce turnover, and drive high performance.

5. **Diversity and Inclusion**: Promoting diversity and inclusion within the workplace is non-negotiable in 21st century HRM. By fostering an inclusive environment that respects and values differences, HR can tap into a wider pool of talent, increase employee satisfaction, and drive innovation.

6. **Employee Engagement**: HRM plays a pivotal role in enhancing employee engagement, which is fundamental for organizational success. This is achieved by creating a positive work environment, fostering strong employee relationships, recognizing employee achievements, and providing growth opportunities.

7. **Employee Well-being and Health**: Increasingly, HR professionals must prioritize employee well-being and health – a reflection of the modern work culture. HR must implement policies and programs to enhance work-life balance, manage stress, and prevent burnout.

8. **Compliance Management**: Strict adherence to local, state, and federal employment laws and regulations is mandatory. Compliance management minimizes the risk of lawsuits, fines, and reputation damage, and promotes a fair work environment.

9. **Change Management**: As organizations undergo continual change to stay competitive, managing this change becomes a key HRM responsibility. This entails preparing employees for changes and guiding them smoothly through

the transition to minimize resistance and business impact.

10. **Technology Integration**: Technology has transformed HRM, from the use of HRIS (Human Resource Information Systems) for automating routine tasks, to AI for talent acquisition and data analytics for decision-making. Staying abreast with technology is a critical function of modern HRM.

Overall, the strategic functions of HRM have evolved significantly in the 21st century. Today's HR professionals are no longer just administrators, rather they are strategic partners contributing to the organization's broader goals and objectives. As the business environment continues to evolve, so will the roles and responsibilities of HR, reinforcing its position as a vital management function.

Contemporary SHRM: Acme Corporation Case Study

In the year 1999, Acme Corporation stood as a formidable leader in the manufacturing industry. Success seemed inextricably linked to traditional management. A vertical organization where power flowed downwards, and personnel management focused solely on administrative tasks. There was a limited emphasis on employee growth and welfare. Essentially employees were considered an expense rather than an investment.

However, the scenario changed dramatically with the onset of the 21st century. Along with the advent of globalization, technology, and evolving workforce demographics, Acme realized that the traditional methods of operating no longer assured a competitive advantage. Their key to sustainability and growth became strategic human resource management.

Strategic Human Resource Management (SHRM) was a fresh, contemporary management approach focusing on aligning human resource strategy with the overall business goals. Acme recognized that their employees were not just expenses, but valuable assets that could drive the company towards its goals.

The Human Resources (HR) department started transforming into a strategic partner, marking a distinct departure from its administrative role. It started contributing to critical decision-making processes at a strategic level. Activities of HR now included employee engagement, talent management, succession planning, competence development, and fostering an inclusive work culture. Acme embraced change by integrating SHRM, one day at a time. Technology was the bedrock of this change. Automation took over repetitive, mundane tasks, freeing HR to concentrate on strategic roles. By employing artificial intelligence, HR began identifying gaps in skills and providing proactive solutions. It enabled them to forecast workforce needs, comprehend employee sentiments better, and improve overall efficiency.

Acme also accepted the diversity and dynamism of the evolving workforce. Millennials and Generation Z stepped in, seeking more than just monetary compensation. They desired a favorable work culture, flexible schedules, and meaningful work. Acme changed, considering these needs. They focused on fostering a supportive and motivating environment, flexibility, and work-life balance, significantly improving overall employee satisfaction and productivity. Moreover, they emphasized upskilling and reskilling, considering market volatility. They believed in nurturing their employees and equipping them with the skills to meet the dynamic changes in their roles.

Acme Corporation realized, as did many other organizations of the 21st century, that reinforcing the connection between people and the organization is an absolute necessity. As such, they focused on enhancing transparency, trust, and communication – all of which greatly led to increased staff satisfaction and in turn, bolstered loyalty towards the company. Though initially considered a support function, HR became a strong pillar for Acme. The 21st century focused on empowering HR to effectively meet future challenges, making them a strategic partner in the boardroom. HR's evolution from administrative work to focusing on people-centric activities became the highlight.

Overall, the incorporation of SHRM allowed Acme to see their employees as valuable strategic assets and invest in their growth and development happily. Not only did this ensure enhanced employee satisfaction and retention but also an improved bottom line. Through SHRM, Acme succeeded in aligning its people, processes, and systems to contribute to the overall business objectives, thereby becoming a sustainable entity in the 21st-century business landscape.

Contemporary SHRM: A Biblical Perspective

The essence of strategic human resources management (SHRM) involves the formulation and execution of HR strategies that align with the goals and objectives of an organization. While the secular business world remains focused primarily on profit maximization, it is pertinent for Christian organizations and HR practitioners to view and practice HR from a biblical perspective. This perspective transcends pure economic return and considers intrinsic human value and divine principles.

1. Creating Value: Genesis 1:27 (KJV), asserts that "God created mankind in His own image…" This verse underscores the inherent value and worth of every individual. In line with this, HR managers must adopt policies and practices that mirror this understanding of human worth, fostering work environments that affirm dignity, respect, and equality. This approach ultimately encourages a motivated and productive workforce.

2. Leadership & Stewardship: Leadership is a pivotal aspect of SHRM. Leaders are required not only to manage but also to promote Christian values and exemplify biblical principles in their management styles. The biblical admonition of stewardship, 1 Peter 4:10 (KJV) "As every man hath received the gift, even so, minister the same one to another, as good stewards of the manifold grace of God." This biblical passage emphasizes the need for leaders to administer their authority responsibly, ensuring the provision, protection, and development of their staff.

3. Ethics and Justice: The 21st-century business landscape thrives on ethical management practices—an essential principle that resonates with biblical teachings. According to Proverbs 11:1(KJV) "A false balance is abomination to the Lord: but a just weight is his delight." This passage warns against dishonest scales, promoting fair and honest dealings in all transactions. Human Resources practices should thus be governed by a strong commitment to ethical behavior, fairness, and justice.

4. Humility and Service: In Matthew 20:26-28 (KJV) "But it shall not be so among you: but whosoever will be great among you, let him be your minister; And whosoever will be chief among you, let him be your servant: Even as the Son of man came not to be ministered unto, but to minister, and to give his life a ransom for many." In these passages, Jesus Christ presented a model of leadership that is based on humility and service. This model can be particularly impactful in fostering a positive organizational culture where leaders serve not just as bosses but as custodians vested in the development and welfare of their employees.

5. Embracing Diversity: The New Testament promotes the principle of unity in diversity. Galatians 3:28(KJV), denotes that "There is neither Jew nor Greek, there is neither bond nor free, there is neither male nor female: for ye are all one in Christ Jesus." Embracing diversity and championing inclusivity in SHRM aligns with this biblical principle, creating a harmonious workplace that mirrors the kingdom of God.

Implications for Practice:

Indeed, adopting a biblical perspective on SHRM reiterates the need for ethical leadership, respect for human dignity, justice, humility, and service. It transforms the organization, making it not just a revenue-generating entity but a platform for modeling Christ-like behavior. Furthermore, the implementation of these biblical principles in SHRM enhances employee motivation, boosts staff morale, and fosters both individual and organizational growth.

As we navigate through the 21st century, the values of the gospel remain timeless and relevant, providing enduring principles that should guide our strategic human resources management practices. Balancing profitability and adhering to biblical principles is not only feasible but also beneficial. As Christian-HR practitioners, our goal should be to demonstrate God's love and wisdom in our management practices, establishing organizations that are not just successful, but entities that serve as conduits of God's glory.

Chapter 3: Leadership in SHRM: Contemporary Perspective

Leadership is a paramount factor in the strategic growth and development of organizations during the 21st Century. Its role is crucial in SHRM as it directly influences organizational culture, morale, and performance. In the current global, competitive business environment, effective leadership within SHRM can significantly enhance operational efficiency, productivity, and sustainability.

In the 21st Century, leadership in SHRM has undergone rapid transformation due to technological advancement, globalization, demographic changes, and a paradigm shift in work ethics and culture. Traditional hierarchical leadership structures have given way to more inclusive, collaborative, and transformational leadership styles. Leaders are now expected to promote innovation, diversity, and adaptability, while continuously striving for excellence.

Moreover, contemporary HR leaders have a strategic role in aligning HR policies and practices with the organization's vision, mission, and overall business strategy. Leadership in SHRM involves not just managing personnel but shaping organizational capabilities and fostering a conducive work environment. This expands beyond mere recruitment or performance management. It involves actively facilitating employee development, fostering positive employee relations, and ensuring workforce flexibility and resilience.

Strategic HRM Leadership in Practice

In a globally competitive business environment, SHRM leadership implies cultivating a culture that values employee well-being, creativity, diversity, and mutual respect. It is about building a learning organization where employees are encouraged and facilitated to acquire new skills and competencies, thereby directly contributing to organizational agility and competitive advantage.

Importantly, strategic HR leaders need to ensure that HR strategies and interventions align with organizational objectives, anticipate future organizational needs, and leverage the potential of human capital to its fullest. To accomplish this, leaders need to be adept at change management and foster a culture of continuous learning and adaptability.

In essence, SHRM leadership involves the following key areas:

1. **Visionary Leadership**: Formulating and communicating a clear strategic direction for the HR function in line with the organizational goals.

2. **Advocacy**: Representing the interests of employees as strategic partners, while aligning their capabilities with the strategic needs of the organization.

3. **Talent Management**: Developing robust systems for identifying, attracting, developing, and retaining talent, while building a culture of competence, commitment, and contribution.

4. **Change management**: Managing change proactively and constructively, creating a resilient and adaptive organization.

5. **Diversity and Inclusion**: Promoting diversity and inclusion as a source of innovation, creativity, and sustainable competitiveness.

Overall, leadership in contemporary SHRM presents both opportunities and challenges. By fostering a visionary, inclusive, and strategic approach to HRM, leaders can significantly enhance organizational capability, competitiveness, and sustainability in the complex and dynamic 21st-century business landscape. It is no longer about managing people; it's about leading a strategic function that catalyzes organizational growth and success.

Contemporary SHRM Leadership: Apex Ltd. Case Study

In the heart of New York City, nestled amongst towering skyscrapers lay the headquarters of a globally recognized corporation – Apex Ltd. Apex had been a market leader in the technology industry for years. However, by the onset of the 21st century, the company started witnessing a plateau in its profit margins and employee productivity. The board of directors soon recognized that this lull represented not a market challenge, but rather an internal leadership crisis requiring a strategic Human Resources pivot.

    Apex's HR department was traditionally viewed as a rather transactional entity, providing necessary but not strategic or leadership-driven functions like payroll, benefits administration, and resolving minor employee issues. However, by the 21st century, this approach towards HRM was becoming increasingly outdated. Businesses worldwide were fast recognizing the need for dynamic, adaptable leadership in HR roles – leadership that would redefine corporate strategies considering changing tech trends, diverse workforces, and globalized operations.

Recognizing this need for change, Apex's board appointed a new CHRO – Zoe Keller. Keller, known for her transformational leadership approach, immediately set about restructuring the company's HR management. She brought a strategic vision to her role, recognizing that in the contemporary business landscape, dynamic leadership and an integrated HR strategy were key to rejuvenating Apex's corporate performance.

More than just implementing policies, Keller saw her role as creating a culture that linked HR procedures with the company's overarching business strategy, thus aligning individual employee performance with Apex's corporate goals. She exhibited a leadership style that values transparency, inclusivity, and data-driven decision-making. She introduced a comprehensive performance management system that factored in workforce analytics, thus creating a climate of performance-based rewards that directly tied into individual employee's contributions to the company's objectives.

Another primary area Keller revolutionized was Apex's learning and development programs. Recognizing the rapid digitalization of the tech sector, Keller aimed to foster a culture of continuous learning within Apex. She deployed several upskilling initiatives that, when combined with Apex's performance management system, ensured constant employee growth parallel to company growth.

Similarly, recognizing the increasingly diverse and global nature of 21st-century workforces, Keller introduced flexible working policies and inclusive employee engagement initiatives. These initiatives increased Apex's appeal to global talent while fostering a nurturing, adaptable corporate culture. By directly addressing employee concerns, something previous leaders failed to do, Keller became a beacon of empathy and transparency at Apex, earning her team's trust, and building a more engaged workforce dedicated to achieving company goals.

Under Keller's transformative leadership, Apex Ltd.'s human resources management underwent a strategic overhaul to become a competitive advantage on the global stage. Not only did company performance revive, but employee engagement and overall satisfaction also skyrocketed. Keller's story, therefore, reinforces the transformative potential of leadership in 21st-century strategic human resources management. Today, Apex Ltd stands as a testament to the fact that dynamic and strategic HR leadership is not a mere option, but a necessity for contemporary organizational success.

Contemporary SHRM Leadership: A Biblical Perspective

The biblical view of leadership presents a paradigm that is highly relevant and applicable in contemporary human resource management. This perspective posits leadership as a service meant to enhance the well-being of others, rather than as a vehicle to attain personal aspiration. The influence of this guiding principle becomes apparent when we analyze and apply it within the scope of 21st-century strategic human resources management.

In 21st-century strategic human resource management, leaders are expected to be visionary, transformative, adaptable, and empathetic. Within this context, biblical teachings provide a valuable framework. For instance, the servant leader model presented in the Bible (Mark 10:43-44, KJV) aligns with the idea of leadership in contemporary human resource management. The perspective that 'whosoever of you will be the chiefest, shall be servant of all' promotes a leadership style keenly attentive to the needs and challenges of the workforce, thereby serving as a strategic tool in galvanizing productive, fulfilled, and loyal employees.

Furthermore, the Bible encourages the development of diverse skills and talents (Romans

12:4-8, KJV). This echoes the HR management's understanding that each employee brings unique talents and skills to the table which should be recognized, developed, and utilized. Considering a drastically changing business landscape, leaders are tasked with the responsibility of fostering an environment that values diversity and inclusion, encourages continuous learning, and aligns employee growth with organizational goals.

The principle of fairness and integrity, as described in Proverbs 11:1, also provides valuable insights for 21st-century HR management. The verse, 'A false balance is abomination to the Lord: but a just weight is his delight' underscores the need for ethical behavior, fairness, and integrity in all dealings. This aligns with the current HR focus on ethical leadership and equitable treatment of all employees. By incorporating this principle, HR management can foster trust, build credibility, and enhance the overall organizational culture.

Finally, the biblical concept of responsible stewardship also has a critical place in contemporary human resource management. Leaders are not just leaders; they are stewards entrusted with human resources. The Parable of the Talents (Matthew 25:14-30, KJV) underscores the responsibility of leaders to maximize the potential of their followers, adding significant value to their lives and the organization.

Interestingly, the biblical perspective on leadership offers timeless principles that can significantly enhance strategic human resource management in the 21st-century business context. To achieve success and resilience in an ever-changing global environment, organizations must incorporate these biblically rooted principles that emphasize servant leadership, talent management, fairness, stewardship, and mutual respect.

Chapter 4: Organizational Strategy in Contemporary SHRM

In the rapidly changing business environment of the 21st century, the importance of integrating organizational strategy with SHRM has intensified. To achieve long-term sustainability and maintain a competitive edge, organizations must align their human resource (HR) functions with the overarching corporate strategy. This strategic shift in HRM structures refers to the transition from traditional, operationally focused HR approaches to more proactive, strategic tactics engrained within the fabric of an organization's planning processes.

A strategic approach to HRM entails viewing the organization's workforce as more than mere implementers of management's instructions - they are valuable contributors to organizational success. The key tenets of SHRM focus on the quest for competitive advantage through the effective management of the organization's human capital and aligning HR strategy with business strategy.

The strategic alignment of HRM can be realized through the adoption of several HRM practices that contribute to meeting organizational objectives. These include talent management, where the organization identifies key roles that contribute to business strategy and ensure they are appropriately filled with competent personnel; and performance management, where organizations adopt well-crafted systems to monitor and evaluate performance, reward excellence, and address underperforming assets.

The rise of globalization, technology advancements, and the shift toward knowledge-based economies have driven the need for more strategic HR functions. In this era, organizations must be adaptable to succeed. Consequently, adaptability should not only be reflected in the company's strategies and practices but also its HR. A robust strategic human resource management system will support this needed flexibility.

In the 21st century, integrating SHRM with organizational strategy also demands attention to external factors, such as market trends, competitor behavior, and cultural attributes. It is the role of contemporary HR professionals to incorporate these diverse external pressures into the organization's HR strategy, harmonizing the workforce with the shifting business environment. Consequently, HR professionals need to foresee business trends and design HR tactics that not only address these trends but propel the organization ahead of its competitors.

Further, organizations must also ensure that their SHRM practices promote ethical behavior and corporate social responsibility. In an era defined by increased transparency and public scrutiny, an organization's reputation hinges on the ethical conduct of its workforce. Accountability, fairness, and respect should be embedded in HR policies to maintain a strong ethical reputation.

The integration of organizational strategy with strategic human resource management is not optional in the modern business environment. It is a critical component of strategic planning that enables organizations to leverage their human capital advantageously. Keeping pace with the evolution of business dynamics, HR strategies should be transformed and realigned continuously with the business objectives. This will provide organizations with a resilient and adaptable workforce, capable of driving the organization into future growth and profitability.

Forethought, flexibility, ethical consideration, and strategic alignment are indispensable elements of an effective contemporary HRM structure. As organizations navigate the complex landscape of the 21st century, intertwining these elements with organizational strategies will undoubtedly yield remarkable results.

Organizational Strategy in Contemporary SHRM: TechTonic & Apex HR Case Study

Once upon a time in the technology-driven world of the 21st century, an organization named

'TechTonic' realized the growing demands of their industry. To stay competitive and thrive, TechTonic needed a strategic approach to its Human Resources Management. They sought the assistance of a prestigious HR Consultancy firm, Apex HR, specializing in transformative human resource strategies.

    Apex HR began by understanding the unique organizational strategy of TechTonic, assessing their existing HR practices, and the external business environment. They found TechTonic's pillars were innovation, customer-centricity, and agility. To align the human resource practices with these guiding principles, Apex HR proposed a Strategic Human Resources Management (SHRM) plan. This plan focused on harnessing the potential of human capital to fuel TechTonic's key strategies and ensuring the team's skills, knowledge, and abilities were appropriately aligned with the future growth of the organization.

A key change was establishing a performance-based culture that rewarded innovation customer orientation and customer-orientation. The appraisal system was revamped to include metrics aligned with the company's strategic goals. This led to a motivated workforce, striving to contribute to the strategic objectives of the business.

As an integral part of SHRM, a learning and development program was installed to equip employees with the latest tools and technology trends. This program not only enhanced their skills but also created a pool of adaptable and flexible workers, a highly valued asset in the rapidly evolving technology industry.

Another pillar of their SHRM was a robust talent management strategy. Apex HR stressed the necessity of not just attracting the best talent but also retaining them. This included nurturing a positive work environment, competitive remuneration packages, and scope for personal and professional growth. This strategic approach ensured that TechTonic had a strong team of committed, skilled workforce that added value to their operations.

Tied closely with talent management was succession planning. TechTonic was guided in identifying and preparing future leaders within the organization who were equipped to handle strategic roles. This ensured that even in the event of unexpected departures, the organization would not get disrupted.

The results of redefined HR strategies were clearly visible in TechTonic's performance, reflected by increased overall productivity, lower employee turnover, and improved financial performance. It displayed the power of strategic human resource management in transforming TechTonic from failing to thriving. This tale of TechTonic serves as a paradigm of contemporary 21st-century SHRM. It showcases the transformative power of a strategic human resources approach and its critical role in the successful execution of organizational strategy.

HR plays a strategic partner role in today's fast-changing business landscape, aligning talent and business strategies to drive performance and growth. As demonstrated in TechTonic's story, effective strategic human resources management is an integral element in shaping the success saga of 21st-century organizations.

Organizational Strategy in Contemporary SHRM: A Biblical Perspective

Foundational to biblical teaching is the principle of stewardship, that all we have has been entrusted to us by God for purposes beyond our interests. This perspective, coupled with the principles of love, integrity, and service, can provide an indispensable framework for developing an effective organizational strategy in modern strategic human resources management. Applying these tenets to the 21st-century professional setting isn't just following ethical guidelines; it's returning to the roots of humanity to foster a workplace that's nurturing, productive, and filled with purpose.

Organizational Strategy & Stewardship:

1 Peter 4:10 (KJV) tells us: "As every man hath received the gift, even so minister the same one to another, as good stewards of the manifold grace of God." This verse emphasizes the responsibility bestowed upon each individual to utilize their talents for communal gain. Likewise, an HR strategic plan that incorporates this stewardship principle may inspire leaders and employees to use their strengths, skills, and knowledge for the benefit of the entire organization. Leaders, in their strategic planning, must strive to create an environment that optimizes these resources and encourages individuals to give their best, fostering a sense of shared purpose in line with the organizational vision.

Integrity In HR Practices

Proverbs 11:3 (KJV) teaches "The integrity of the upright shall guide them: but the perverseness of transgressors shall destroy them." In SHRM, integrity catalyzes trust within the workplace, which is fundamental for employee engagement, productivity, and loyalty. For leadership, this means providing reliable guidance and moral behavior that employees can emulate. For HR, this could translate into developing fair and transparent policies and practices that follow not just the letter of the law, but also its spirit, encapsulating the moral fibers of truth, justice, and fairness.

Love and Service

Mark 12:31 (KJV) states: "...Thou shalt love thy neighbour as thyself..." On a corporate level, loving your neighbor can be expressed through care for employees' welfare, empathy in dealing with their concerns, and prioritizing their career development. Strategic HR management needs to foster a culture where employees feel valued, understood, and considered. This also extends to service; the primary calling for Christians is to serve others. In HR, this might materialize in the form of servant leadership, where leaders prioritize the growth and welfare of their team over their ambitions.

Fostering an organizational strategy that integrates biblical principles allows for a more holistic approach, leveraging the spiritual dimension of human nature for the greater good of the organization. By focusing on stewardship, integrity, love, and service, HR can usher in transformational leadership that positively impacts not just the employees, but also the organization, its stakeholders, and society at large.

As we navigate the complexities of 21st-century HR management, these timeless principles serve as guiding lights, underlining the importance of moral and ethical behavior in a contemporary, fast-paced business environment.

Chapter 5: Performance Management in Contemporary SHRM

Performance management is a critical function in the strategic management of human resources in today's business environment. With organizations operating in an age of rapid technological advancement, globalization, and changing work patterns, an effective performance management system is an indispensable tool to drive organizational performance and achieve strategic objectives.

Performance management systems have evolved from traditional appraisals and evaluations to comprehensive systems integrating feedback, coaching, and learning opportunities. In the 21st century, they have become an ongoing, dynamic process that aligns an organization's mission, goals, and objectives with the performance, skills, and development of its employees.

In the modern business world, the strategic role of HR has gained considerable importance. Human resources are now viewed not merely as an administrative function, but as a strategic partner that contributes to the organization's success. HRM strategies now revolve around attracting, retaining, and developing talent that will provide a competitive advantage.

In this context, performance management helps to identify top performers, provide constructive feedback, set reasonable performance expectations, and address underperformance. It also fosters a performance-oriented culture within the organization.

Moreover, technology plays a significant role in shaping performance management practices. Advances in HRM software and analytics have made it possible for businesses to monitor performance in real-time, track progress toward goals, and gain insights into potential gaps that need to be addressed.

A contemporary performance management system also places a strong emphasis on development. It recognizes that improved performance is tied closely to learning and development opportunities. Thus, such a system encourages ongoing coaching and feedback, offers training and development programs, and facilitates career progression and succession planning.

Incorporating diversity and inclusion in performance management is another trend in strategic HRM. Research shows that organizations that are diverse and inclusive tend to exhibit better performance. In this regard, performance management systems have to ensure that performance benchmarks are equitable, and assessments are unbiased.

Effective performance management is crucial for maintaining employee engagement and motivation. It gives employees a clear understanding of their roles and expectations, provides them with constructive feedback, and rewards them for their performance. Moreover, it enhances their job satisfaction and loyalty to the organization.

Thus, in the 21st century, SHRM must focus on developing, implementing, and updating performance management systems that align with the organization's goals and the dynamic changes in the business world. This will require integrating advanced technology, fostering a performance-oriented culture, encouraging continuous learning and development, promoting diversity and inclusion, and nurturing employee engagement and satisfaction.

To encapsulate, performance management is no longer just about monitoring employee performance; it has become a strategic tool that drives organizational success in the competitive and complex 21st-century business environment.

Performance Management in Contemporary SHRM: Company XYZ Case Study

In today's fast-paced business environment, performance management has evolved into a strategic pillar in modern HR practices. Understanding the transformation in performance management strategies can be beneficial for business leaders, HR professionals, and organizations at large. This case study examines the application of Performance Management through an in-depth examination of Company XYZ, a leading global brand in the e-commerce industry.

Company XYZ, despite being a relatively young entrant in the e-commerce sector, outshone its competition by achieving a customer base of millions and an impressive sales turnover. The HR department identified the need to sustain this momentum through a strategic performance management system that focused on continuous improvement, feedback, and motivation.

Company XYZ implemented a performance management system that accentuated constant feedback, individual and team key performance indicators (KPIs) and ensured alignment with overall business goals. The KPIs and the objectives were clear, measurable, and tailored according to each employee's role. Recognizing the potential of technology, the company employed sophisticated HR software that provided real-time performance metrics and a clear visualization of each employee's contribution to strategic business objectives.

The initial challenge was the employees' resistance to the new system as they felt continuously monitored. It led to a period of adjustment and a need for HR to facilitate frequent open discussions and training sessions until employees were comfortable using the system.

Over time, the continuous feedback system resulted in constructive communication between the managers and the employees. Employees appreciated on-the-spot recognition and prompt remediation of issues. Compliance to KPIs improved, and employees understood their contribution to the overall success of the business. By tracking performance, identifying training needs, and rewarding performance, the system has improved Company XYZ's output and productivity significantly.

Company XYZ's case demonstrates that performance management in the 21st century has shifted from the traditional annual review system to a more continuous, integrated, and strategic approach. The understanding that performance management is a holistic, ongoing process is central to this shift. Through a successful performance management system, companies can align individual goals with strategic business objectives, thereby driving organizational performance and productivity.

This case study underscores the transformed landscape of performance management practices, bearing lessons for any organization seeking to harness the full potential of its workforce in the strategic HR role.

Performance Management in Contemporary SHRM:

A Biblical Perspective

Performance management, a critical component of strategic human resource management, focuses on ensuring individual employee performance aligns with the organization's strategic objectives. The Bible, considered an essential source of wisdom and guidance, offers several perspectives that are relevant to contemporary performance management practice.

First, one crucial aspect of performance management is fairness and integrity, which are principles emphasized throughout the scriptures. For example, in Proverbs 11:1 (KJV), it is written, "A false balance is abomination to the Lord: but a just weight is his delight." This principle is a direct analog to performance management, where the accurate assessment of an employee's performance is vital. Moreover, an organization influenced by biblical teaching would be obligated to destroy any bias in performance assessment to ensure that all employees are treated equally and fairly.

Second, feedback and correction are fundamental performance management aspects, and these are also topics highlighted in the Bible.

Proverbs 27:17 (KJV) states, "Iron sharpeneth iron; so a man sharpeneth the countenance of his friend." An organizational perspective might view this as the potential for continuous improvement in employees via constructive feedback and knowledge sharing. Similarly, Hebrews 12:11 (KJV) points out, "Now no chastening for the present seemeth to be joyous, but grievous: nevertheless afterward it yieldeth the peaceable fruit of righteousness unto them which are exercised thereby." It suggests that constructive criticism, while difficult in the short term, can lead to long-term individual and organizational growth.

Third, motivation and reward systems are essential performance management strategies, resonating with the concept of reaping what you sow from Galatians 6:7 (KJV) - "Be not deceived;

God is not mocked: for whatsoever a man soweth, that shall he also reap." It implies that employees who put in effort and contribute significantly to the organization will reap the rewards. Consequently, organizations should have a comprehensive and fair reward system reflective of individual contributions.

Lastly, results-oriented performance management echoes the Biblical focus on deeds, outcomes, and results. James 2:26 (KJV) states, "For as the body without the spirit is dead, so faith without works is dead also." This promotes the concept of assessing an employee based on outputs and results rather than merely intentions or effort exerted.

Interestingly, this Biblical perspective offers significant insights that affirm and enrich modern performance management. The principles of fairness, feedback, motivation, and results orientation can be seamlessly integrated into an organization's strategic HR management. It highlights the ongoing relevance of scripture, providing a moral and ethical compass that can guide 21st-century organizations in treating their employees with fairness, dignity, and respect.

Chapter 6: Talent Management in Contemporary SHRM

With the advent of the 21st century, the corporate landscape has witnessed a dynamic shift specifically in the sphere of SHRM. This evolution is spearheaded by the strategic realization of the inherent value that employees bring to the table. The contemporary corporate scenario recognizes employees no longer as mere resources but as 'talent' that needs to be effectively managed to gain a competitive edge.

Building a robust Talent Management Strategy has thus emerged as a quintessential facet of 21st-century SHRM. This framework seeks to attract, retain, and develop skilled and talented individuals to ensure the sustained growth and success of a corporation.

A crucial element of this strategic approach is acquiring the right talent. Firms are expanding their traditional recruitment horizons and venturing into online and social media platforms. With the global talent pool at their disposal, organizations are rooting for quality rather than quantity. The aim is to not just to fill a vacant spot, but to acquire individuals possessing the skills, experience, and values that align with the company's vision and culture.

As the episodic era of lifetime employment fades into obscurity, retaining top talent poses its own set of challenges. Firms are becoming more attuned to the needs and aspirations of their workforce to curtail rapid turnover. They are creating an exhilarating work environment, offering life-insurance, healthcare benefits, work-from-home flexibility, performance rewards, and much more to incentivize their stay.

Integral to talent management is the ongoing development and enhancement of employee talent. Through performance reviews, training, coaching, and mentorship programs, organizations are investing in honing the skills of their workforce, grooming them for leadership roles, and essentially preparing them for the future. This not only helps in the career progression and personal growth of the employees but also enhances their commitment and loyalty towards the organization.

Moreover, the realization that high employee engagement results in increased productivity and profitability has resulted in its incorporation within strategic HRM. Utilizing feedback systems, communication tools, and engagement programs, companies are fostering an atmosphere of recognition, trust, and respect, ultimately leading to increased job satisfaction.

Undoubtedly, the criticality of data in this digital age cannot be overstated. Data analytics-powered decision-making is replacing traditional gut-feel decisions. From predicting talent trends, gauging employee performance, and churn rate to discerning training needs, data analytics is reshaping SHRM. It helps corporations in making informed decisions to deliver bespoke employee experiences, thus retaining, and attracting top talent.

The holistic concept of Talent Management is rapidly becoming the cornerstone of 21st-century SHRM. The strategic transition from managing 'human resources' to administering 'talent' delineates the transformation of HRM in the contemporary business world. This innovative approach encapsulates the inclusive journey from talent acquisition to retention and development, thus fostering a productive and engaging work culture. This, in turn, impetus enhanced corporate performance, innovation, and long-term success amid an increasingly competitive business landscape.

Talent Planning in Contemporary SHRM: AdaptiByte Case Study

In the 21st-century business landscape, the importance of strategic human resources management cannot be overstated, for it plays an indispensable role in empowering organizations to tackle the uncertainties of today's fast-moving business world. Central to strategic human resources management is the concept of 'Talent

Planning,' a proactive and systematic process of identifying, developing, and retaining a workforce that is capable, motivated, and aligned with the organization's strategic objectives.

In the past, human resources management was often viewed as a reactive, administrative function. However, with the demands of the 21st century, organizations are recognizing the necessity to shift to a more strategic approach, pivoting their focus on talent planning to gain a competitive advantage. This new realignment entails identifying the right people, with the right skills, at the right time and placing them in the right job to achieve the company's strategic objectives.

A prime example of talent planning in action can be seen in a high-tech global company, AdaptiByte Enterprises, stepping into the 21st century with a struggling product portfolio and low employee engagement. Recognizing the need for change, the new leadership decided to employ strategic human resources planning to reinvigorate and realign its workforce. New strategic objectives were set with future technological trends in mind, pushing innovation to the forefront of its organizational goals.

The first step for AdaptiByte was to identify the skills and competencies that would be required to achieve these goals. A new skill matrix was created, laying the foundation for potential talent acquisition. Simultaneously, a thorough analysis was conducted of existing staff, identifying high potential, skill gaps, and developmental needs. To align the current workforce with these needs, extensive re-skilling and upskilling programs were introduced, which not only boosted morale but also increased the adaptability of their staff. A motivation-centric culture was promoted, taking into consideration the shift towards value-driven employment expectations in the new era.

In parallel, the talent acquisition strategy was revamped. The company developed a competency-based recruitment process to ensure that new hires matched the skill matrix, were cultural fits, and had the potential to contribute to long-term objectives. A diverse talent pool was targeted, acknowledging the link between diversity and innovation, and enhancing the company's global competitiveness.

Moreover, to retain its valuable human assets, AdaptiByte introduced competitive and flexible reward strategies tailored to individual needs. Career progression paths were clear, offering a future-forward perspective to employees and fostering their loyalty to the company. As a result of these strategic changes, AdaptiByte Enterprises witnessed a dramatic turnaround. Employee engagement levels soared, product innovation excelled, and business performance outperformed industry standards - reflective of the power of strategic human resources management.

Overall, talent planning in the 21st century is an integral pillar of SHRM. It requires a forward-thinking approach, ensuring a workforce that is prepared and empowered to navigate the challenges of the modern business world. As the AdaptiByte case illustrates, organizations that prioritize talent planning position themselves to thrive amidst the challenges of the 21st century, driving sustainable success via their greatest asset - their people.

Talent Planning in Contemporary SHRM: A Biblical Perspective

Talent planning is an integral part of strategic human resource management (SHRM), particularly in the contemporary 21st-century business landscape characterized by technological advancement, heightened competition, and demographic changes. Integrating a biblical perspective into our understanding and approach to talent planning can offer profound insights into the values, principles, and ethics that ought to inform our human resource (HR) strategies.

According to Biblical teachings, every human being is 'created in the image of God' (Genesis 1:27, KJV), thus inherently valuable. As such, they represent a vital resource whose creative and productive potential needs to be unlocked and nurtured. In the context of talent planning, this underscores the importance of businesses recognizing and capitalizing on the unique capabilities of every employee rather than treating human resources as just another business asset.

The Parable of Talents in Matthew 25:14-30 (KJV) is particularly instructive for talent planning. In this parable, the servants are given different measures of talent (money) and are expected to utilize and multiply them. The two servants who make profitable use of their talents are commended while the one who fails to do so is reprimanded. Drawing parallels between the Biblical 'talents' and the modern workplace 'talents' (skills and capabilities), this parable offers two critical lessons.

Firstly, every individual possesses unique talents which, when effectively harnessed and developed, can generate significant value. As HR professionals, we bear the responsibility of identifying, nurturing, and effectively allocating these talents in a way that optimizes the overall organizational performance – much like the Master expected his servants to multiply the talents entrusted to them.

Secondly, it highlights the principle of accountability. Just as the servants were accountable for the talents given to them, HR professionals, managers, and workers must bear responsibility for the talents under their charge. This encompasses finding and recruiting talented individuals, facilitating their professional and personal growth, and ensuring their talents are being utilized in a way that drives both individual and organizational success.

Another key biblical principle that ought to guide talent planning is fairness and equality. While the bible acknowledges the diversity in individual talents (1 Corinthians 12:4-7, KJV), it underscores the equality of all members of the body of Christ (Galatians 3:28, KJV). As such, talent management should not unfairly favor one group or individual at the expense of others. Instead, it should ensure equitable opportunities for all employees to develop and use their talents – fostering an inclusive organizational culture that values diversity.

Overall, the essence of SHRM and talent planning, from a Biblical perspective, is rooted in the value and unique capabilities that everyone brings to the workplace, the principle of accountability in managing these talents, and the commitment to fairness and equality in the process. Incorporating these insights into 21st-century HR practices is not only consistent with ethical ideals but also aligns with contemporary HR strategies aimed at promoting diversity, inclusion, and comprehensive talent development.

Chapter 7: Mergers & Acquisitions (M&A) and Contemporary SHRM

Mergers and Acquisitions (M&As) have become an inherent part of the global corporate landscape in the 21st century. They are perceived as a critical growth strategy by many organizations, aiming at market expansion, diversification, acquisition of new technologies, or competition eradication. Herein, the strategic role of Human Resources (HR) in managing M&As effectively is of utmost importance.

M&As constitute a period of significant change for organizations, with implications for varied organizational processes and stakeholders. It involves an amalgamation or restructuring of cultures, systems, processes, and people. In the face of these disruptions, the role of HR expands beyond traditional employee management.

Strategic HR management aims at aligning HR policies and practices with overall business strategies, enabling better realization of merger objectives.

Firstly, HR can play a critical role in the due diligence process. The cultural, human capital, and organizational capabilities should be thoroughly analyzed. Any disparities in cultures or work ethics between the merging entities can lead to post-merger integration problems. HR, with its insights and expertise, can adeptly identify and address these pre-emptively.

Secondly, the integration phase is riddled with complexities as it involves unifying the policies, systems, and schemes of two organizations. This requires strategic decision-making relating to the retainment or merger of distinct HRM systems, pay structures, and job designs to adapt to new organizational realities. This phase can cause anxiety among employees, possibly affecting their performance or leading to higher attrition rates. HR must, therefore, devise and implement effective communication strategies to clarify uncertainties and ensure a smooth transition.

Thirdly, HR plays a significant part in fostering a new organizational culture. This can involve harnessing positive aspects from each entity's culture and infusing them to create a new shared identity. Maintaining transparent communication, promoting leadership behaviors, strategically managing change, and initiating team-building efforts can significantly influence the collective psyche of employees, creating a more cohesive and synergistic workforce.

Lastly, M&As are accompanied by staff reductions to eliminate role duplicity and achieve cost efficiencies. HR must manage this redistributive process with utmost fairness and transparency, mitigating the emanating emotional and motivational challenges. Additionally, the decision of who remains, who leaves, and who assumes new roles should be dealt with strategically, keeping in mind the future business directions and talent requirements.

The role of HR in M&As extends beyond traditional functions to strategic ones, influencing the seamless transition and ultimate success of these initiatives. It is only through comprehensive due diligence, strategic integration, culture creation, effective communication, and fair staff redistribution that organizations can fully realize the potential gains from M&As.

Contemporary SHRM and M&A: A Case Study of Acme Ltd. and Biopharma Inc.

In the contemporary landscape of the 21st century, strategic human resources management has become more than just hiring, firing, and payroll. It has evolved to play an integral role in the planning and implementation of organizational strategies, particularly in mergers and acquisitions (M&A). Mergers and Acquisitions represent significant shifts to an organization's structure and culture. The successful execution of such initiative's rests on a firm grounding in strategic human resources management. Let's delve into a fictitious case that exemplifies the role HR plays in M&A in the 21st century.

Acme Ltd, a pharmaceutical titan, was set to acquire BioPharma Inc., a biotech startup focusing on genome research. This acquisition was not just an asset purchase, but a move to infuse Acme Ltd.'s line of research with the innovative techniques BioPharma Inc. was known for. Here, the human resource comes into play.

During the due diligence phase, Acme Ltd.'s HR team was given the task of exploring the talent pool of BioPharma Inc. Framing the right questions - recognizing the crucial human components, understanding the organizational culture, and identifying the key personnel that brought value to BioPharma Inc., became vital. The HR team assessed the human factor's worth and the potential cultural clash following the acquisition, contributing to decisions that were both tactical and strategic.

Post-acquisition, when BioPharma Inc. became a subsidiary of Acme Ltd., the HR team faced the herculean task of managing change and harmonizing two distinct corporate cultures. They conducted extensive workshops and training sessions for employees of both organizations, helping them understand and assimilate to the change. They carried out a comprehensive job mapping exercise, ensured the placement of employees in the new structure without bias, and worked on salary harmonization, all with a balanced and rational approach. This not only averted large-scale employee discontent and potential turnovers but also provided transparent and equitable solutions.

In addition, HR was the mediator between the employees and the management, providing clear, regular, and truthful communication from management, assuaging fears, and anxiety, and guiding them through the period of change. Six months later, the employees of both organizations worked amicably without misalignment, the productivity returned to pre-acquisition levels and even surpassed it in some sectors. The transition was anything but smooth, and without the strategic planning and execution by the HR team, it would have been an uphill struggle.

This story is representational of the role of HR in modern M&As. It encapsulates the challenges faced and how HR has advanced in its function from administrative to strategic. The field of HR has come to recognize that employees are more than just human capital but are the soul and driving force of any organization. Recognizing this, and adopting HRM strategies in line with this understanding, makes the difference between successful and failed M&As. In modern M&A strategic HRM is taking center stage. By addressing due diligence, change management, communication, HR policy standardization, and integration, HR specialists can ensure a relatively smooth transition during M&A and help the organization achieve its strategic and operational goals.

M&A and Contemporary SHRM: A Biblical Perspective

The 21st century has seen a significant rise in mergers and acquisitions (M&A) in enterprises globally. As strategic HR professionals, the quest to maximize synergies and achieve organizational efficiency is a common motive. However, this operational paradigm often leaves in its wake, challenging human resources questions about integration, interpersonal relationships, and value systems. It is relevant, therefore, to explore a biblical perspective on these situations to better inform our HR management approaches.

1 Corinthians 12:12-27 (KJV) presents an understanding of the body's interdependence, equally applicable to modern M&A. As the body has many parts, each with unique roles, organizations are also composed of distinct departments. Paul teaches that despite their variation in function, all these parts are critical and complementary for overall growth. HR managers should hold this concept of interdependence at the forefront, allowing it to guide how mergers and acquisitions are managed, particularly the integration phase. Strategic HR integration should not only combine organizations but also create a sense of unity, integrating hearts and minds with the conviction that every employee, regardless of their rank or responsibilities, is vital and has a role to play in the success of the combined entity.

Another biblical principle of relevance is found in Proverbs 16:8 (KJV), which places integrity over wealth. During M&As, it is not uncommon for some organizations to compromise on ethical and moral considerations in pursuit of financial gains. As 21st-century HR managers, this proverb encourages prioritizing integrity. This could mean protecting employee rights, being transparent about changes, and maintaining fair practices in the face of pressure to compromise for the sake of expedience or profit.

Respecting dignity and denying discrimination is a significant cornerstone in Bible teachings. The application of this principle in the light of 21st-century strategic HR management, especially in situations involving M&As, cannot be overstated. Galatians 3:28 (KJV) states: "There is neither Jew nor Greek, there is neither bond nor free, there is neither male nor female: for ye are all one in Christ Jesus." Long-standing prejudices regarding gender, race, religion, or culture should not influence the processes of M&As and the subsequent integration or restructuring that may occur.

Lastly, Matthew 7:12 (KJV) "Therefore all things whatsoever ye would that men should do to you, do ye even so to them: for this is the law and the prophets." This passage encourages us to treat others as we would like to be treated. In an M&A system, this principle may guide the HR management approach towards layoffs and severance packages, providing robust communication lines about future changes and ensuring fairness in restructuring decisions. To navigate the complexities of M&As successfully, modern HR managers should ensure interdependence, value integrity, encourage unity, respect all regardless of status or identity, and treat others kindly and fairly. These biblical principles can offer a timeless, relevant perspective to guide HR decisions, fostering an M&A environment that is not only financially sound but morally and ethically upright. The right fusion of practical HR knowledge with Biblical wisdom offers a balanced approach to making decisions that are both strategically sound and ethically responsible, which eventually leads to more successful outcomes of Mergers and Acquisitions.

Chapter 8: Learning and Development in Contemporary SHRM

In the contemporary corporate sector, with an increasingly competitive, complex, and ever-evolving business environment, Strategic Human Resource Management (SHRM) has gained unprecedented importance. It has become indispensable in aligning individual objectives and organizational goals, essentially aiding in overall business sustainability, growth, and competitiveness. One of the critical components of SHRM is Learning and Development (L&D), playing a vital role in this strategic alignment.

Today's business environment is characterized by constant flux - rapid advancements in technology, frequent market changes, evolving customer demands, and globalization of economies, to name a few. These factors necessitate the need for organizations to have a workforce that is flexible, adaptable, and skilled to navigate through these changes. This is where the role of L&D comes into the limelight.

L&D is essentially focused on improving the knowledge, skills, and abilities (KSAs) of the employees, molding them to fit the organizational purposes better. It is about creating a talent pool that can quickly adapt to new technologies and strategies, understand, and respond to market changes, improve productivity and efficiency, and contribute more effectively to the organization's bottom line.

Strategic integration of L&D initiatives with HRM has a two-pronged advantage. Firstly, it helps in identifying and closing skills gaps, a critical challenge faced by many organizations today. By providing the necessary training and development opportunities, organizations can ensure their employees are well-equipped to meet current as well as future demands.

Secondly, it aids in retaining and engaging employees. Today's workforce values opportunities for personal and professional growth. By focusing on L&D, organizations can show commitment to their employee's growth, thereby improving their job satisfaction, motivation, and overall engagement, ultimately leading to lower turnover rates.

However, it is crucial to note that L&D strategies should not be implemented in isolation. It needs to be part of the broader SHRM and align with the overall organizational strategy. This will ensure that L&D initiatives are not frivolous but targeted toward enhancing those skills and competencies that are of strategic importance to the organization.

Furthermore, the assessment and evaluation of L&D initiatives are equally critical. Regular monitoring of these programs can help evaluate their effectiveness, identify areas for improvement, and ensure a return on investment.

Overall, L&D has emerged as a strategic tool in the realm of Human Resource Management. It can act as a catalyst for enhancing competency, agility, innovation, and engagement within organizations. The onus now lies on how HRM can strategically implement and manage L&D initiatives, driving their effectiveness and ensuring they deliver real value to the organization.

Harnessing L&D in Contemporary SHRM: A Case Study on Tech Spark

In today's SHRM, Learning and Development (L&D) has taken center stage, morphing the roles and responsibilities of HR professionals into catalysts for organizational growth and development. This shift is deeply inspired by the contemporary business environment characterized by rapid technological changes, globalization, and an evolving workforce. Learning has become a lifelong endeavor and organizations that leverage this have become more competitive and proactive.

Take, for instance, Tech Spark - an emerging tech company in Silicon Valley. From its inception, its HR team has been instrumental in fostering a culture of continuous learning. The HR department recognized early in its development that for the organization to stay ahead of its competitors, the employees' skills needed to continually evolve.

Indeed, the HR team placed a premium on collectively mastering emergent technologies and industry best practices. This led to the establishment of a robust L&D program. The program facilitated regular training, workshops, and leadership development initiatives. Team members were consistently encouraged to cultivate curiosity, thus turning the organization into a living, breathing entity keen on growth and knowledge.

The strategic alignment of business objectives with L&D programs was one of the key underpinnings for the niche Tech Spark was carving for itself. The L&D programs were concurrent with the company's strategic objectives, hence ensuring employees were oriented towards achieving the company's mission.

Tech Spark's C-suite benefitted from the strategic L&D initiatives too. Amidst the fast-paced market trends, they were able to keep abreast with new insights and innovative leadership practices. Moreover, they became aware of their role in nurturing a learning culture, leading by example for the rest of the ranks.

The subsequent results were apparent. Tech Spark reported increased productivity and performance. The overall employee satisfaction improved as they felt better equipped and triggered to undertake their specified roles. Additionally, the organization experienced reduced employee turnover, attributing it to the deeply ingrained culture of learning opportunities and career advancement.

The Tech Spark journey underscores the need for L&D to feed into the larger organizational strategy. Notably, today's businesses cannot afford to separate the two. As an HR consultant, it's clear that the HR team's role in maintaining and enhancing human capital has never been more paramount. Ultimately, the transformation of HR from a mere supportive role to a strategic partner denotes a remarkable organization's shift in understanding the importance of learning. Incorporating a well-structured L&D program into the HRM strategy, like our friends at Tech Spark, is now more than ever, a key determinant of an organization's development and sustainability in the 21st-century business landscape.

L&D in SHRM: A Biblical Perspective

Developing a cohesive and strategic approach towards human resource management is a quintessential component for organizations in the 21st century. There is a pressing need for organizations to adapt to the ever-evolving business environment, accompanied by the changing competencies and skills demanded in the labor market. In this context, the concept of Learning and Development (L&D) becomes critical. Drawing upon biblical teachings, this section outlines how L&D strategies could be synthesized in contemporary human resource management.

1. **Commitment to Continuous Learning**: Proverbs 9:9 (KJV) states, "Give instruction to a wise man, and he will be yet wiser: teach a just man, and he will increase in learning." This verse

signifies the vital role of continuous learning and growth. Organizations need to develop a culture that encourages continuous learning, innovation, and adaptability as part of their strategic human resource management.

2. **Guided Development**: As vocalized in Psalm 32:8 (KJV), "I will instruct thee and teach thee in the way which thou shalt go: I will guide thee with mine eye." This passage suggests that organizations should strategize their L&D programs to offer individualized attention, guidance, and mentorship. This ensures employees' skills development aligns with the organizational needs and employees' career development aspirations.

3. **Collaborative Learning**: Ecclesiastes 4:9-10 (KJV) asserts, " Two are better than one; because they have a good reward for their labour. For if

they fall, the one will lift up his fellow: but woe to him that is alone when he falleth; for he hath not another to help him up." These passages promote the concept of collaborative learning. Incorporating collaborative learning strategies such as teamwork, cooperative learning, and peer coaching can foster a supportive work environment and enhance individual employee capabilities and overall organizational productivity.

4. **Emphasizing on Wisdom and Understanding**: Proverbs 24:3-4 (KJV) illustrates, "Through wisdom is a house builded; and by understanding it is established: And by knowledge shall the chambers be filled with all precious and pleasant riches." In L&D terms, wisdom and understanding could be interpreted as skills and competitiveness, highlighting the need

for strategic L&D programs feeding into the knowledge economy. Biblical teachings provide timeless wisdom and guidance that still hold practical value in 21st-century HR practices, especially in shaping effective and strategic learning and development programs. To successfully navigate the dynamic and complex business landscape, organizations should prioritize creating a culture of continuous learning, emphasizing guided development, encouraging collaborative learning, and fostering an understanding that increases wisdom. Following this path in human resource management not only keeps companies at a competitive edge but also promotes a thriving and enriching work environment for their employees.

Chapter 9: Total Rewards in Contemporary SHRM

The confluence of profound shifts in the labor market, and the increasingly discernible impact of the 21st-century technological revolution, has made it inevitable for organizations to reevaluate their present HRM strategies. Chief among the facets of HRM that warrant significant reconsideration is the issue of 'total rewards'.

Total rewards are a contemporary strategic HR concept that refers to the tools and fringe benefits that a company uses to attract, motivate, and retain employees. This includes not just basic salary, but also additional benefits like health insurance, retirement benefits, paid time off, and non-financial incentives like flexible working hours, career development opportunities, and an encouraging work environment. In the present hyper-competitive global marketplace, a well-articulated and effectively implemented total rewards strategy can give a company a strategic advantage and a unique selling proposition in the labor market.

The importance and relevance of total rewards strategies cannot be overstated. For one, the global labor market landscape has evolved dramatically with the proliferation of technology and the Museum of Work. Companies are now dealing with a diverse pool of talent that ranges from full-time employees to freelancers, remote workers, and part-time employees. This diverse workforce, with its distinct expectations and aspirations, necessitates a flexible yet comprehensive total rewards strategy.

Furthermore, the rise of the millennial workforce has compounded the necessity for a more expansive understanding of rewards. This generation, characterized by its quest for work-life balance, personal growth, and meaningful work, demands more than just monetary compensation. Hence, organizations need to rethink their total rewards strategies to not merely include financial compensation and traditional benefits, but also intangible incentives like opportunities for personal growth, the flexibility of the workplace, and the possibility of making meaningful contributions.

An effective total rewards strategy aligns with the organizational goals and culture. For instance, a company that values innovation and risk-taking might reward employees who propose new ideas or take the lead on new projects, potentially motivating others to do the same. In contrast, a company that prioritizes stability and tradition might reward long tenure and consistent performance. Moreover, a compelling rewards strategy must also consider external factors, from local labor laws and market compensation rates to industry trends and the general economic climate. This awareness ensures the organization stays competitive, compliant, and agile amidst shifting circumstances.

Surprisingly, in this 21st-century technological age, successful organizations must adapt and evolve their total rewards strategies. This involves moving away from a one-size-fits-all model to a flexible, personalized approach in line with both the individuals' needs and organizational objectives. Through a comprehensive, well-implemented total rewards strategy, organizations can successfully navigate the complexities of the modern labor market, attracting and retaining the right talent while fostering an engaging, motivational, and productive work environment.

Case Study: Impact of Total Rewards on SHRM

In today's global business environment, the need for robust SHRM is imperative. The prime purpose of SHRM is to ensure that the organization has the human capital it requires to achieve its strategic business objectives. A significant tool within SHRM is "total rewards." This case study will analyze the role and impact of total rewards in contemporary SHRM through the example of a leading global technology firm, Tech Giants Inc. (TGI), which recently redesigned its total rewards program to better align with its new strategic objectives.

Problem Identification

Despite being a successful organization, TGI found its market position threatened by aggressive competitors and rapidly evolving technology trends. Internally, the company was suffering from an alarmingly high turnover rate and dwindling employee engagement. The central assumption was that the employees were not sufficiently motivated or engaged because the existing reward system was not adequately tailored to their needs or the company's strategic objectives.

Intervention

TGI decided to overhaul its total rewards program and align it more closely with the organization's strategic objectives and the employees' aspirations. Total rewards, a concept that extends beyond just salary, incorporating various elements such as benefits, work-life balance, performance recognition, and opportunities for personal development, was seen as a game-changer for the organization. TGI redesigned its total rewards program by offering more flexible work conditions, providing robust healthcare and retirement benefits, increasing the frequency and variety of performance recognition, and investing heavily in personal development and training.

Outcome

After implementing the new total reward program, TGI reported a significant drop in turnover rates – from a high of 22% to an improved 12% within one year. Employee engagement scores rose by 15%, and their annual employee satisfaction survey revealed that the employees felt appreciated and incentivized to perform better. There was a notable enhancement in team performance metrics, and TGI also succeeded in attracting top-tier talent, previously elusive due to its preceding, less competitive rewards system.

Key Learning

This case of TGI underscores the significant impact of the total rewards approach in contemporary SHRM. It highlights the importance of aligning the total rewards system with the strategic objectives - not only to attract, motivate, and retain employees but also to drive performance, enhance engagement, and yield effective business results.

Conclusion

Total rewards are no longer an optional component of SHRM. In an era marked by fierce competition for top talent and rapidly shifting business landscapes, having a total rewards approach that aligns with strategic objectives is indeed indispensable. The case of TGI serves as a strong reminder for HR professionals to continually adapt and align the organization's total rewards in line with the strategic business objectives and the ever-evolving employee expectations. Overall, this case validates the growing importance of a comprehensive and strategic approach to total rewards in the realm of contemporary SHRM.

Total Rewards in Contemporary SHRM: A Biblical Perspective

In the fast-paced, technologically advanced 21st-century business world, strategic human resource management has become a cutting-edge domain. The concept of Total Rewards (TR), a potent strategy to attract, motivate, and retain skilled talent, holds unique relevance. This paper attempts to correlate TR from a biblical perspective where the parables and principles can provide a sound ethical basis for a TR system.

The principles and teachings found in the Bible remain relevant in contemporary society, including the sphere of HRM. One such critical area is the Total Rewards System (TRS), which has evolved as a comprehensive method of bestowing value to employees in return for their work performance and commitment. A Biblical perspective predominantly encourages balancing materialistic and non-material aspects of rewards, fostering an organizational culture where employees feel valued, secure, and supported.

Total Rewards System and Bible Parables:

The parable of the Workers in the Vineyard (Matthew 20: 1-16, KJV) can be perceived as an early form of TR. The vineyard owner rewards all workers equally, emphasizing the importance of fairness and equity, two critical components of a successful TRS.

The teachings from the Parable of the Talents (Matthew 25: 15-30, KJV) imply the association of rewards with performance. Here, the members who showed initiative and generated results were rewarded, laying a foundation for a performance-based rewards system.

Furthermore, the Parable of the Good Samaritan (Luke 10:25-37, KJV) talks about empathy, compassion, and a sense of duty; these morals align with the non-monetary aspects, i.e., fulfillment and personal enrichment, of TR.

Benefits & Investment in Employees:

Proverbs 22:9 (KJV) states, "He that hath a bountiful eye shall be blessed; for he giveth of his bread to the poor." Similarly, a generous TRS signals to the employees that their efforts and contributions are recognized and rewarded appropriately, boosting morale and productivity.

The scripture also talks about investing in employees' growth and betterment. Proverbs 27:17 (KJV) "Iron sharpeneth iron; so a man sharpeneth the countenance of his friend." This passage points to the concept of learning and development, a crucial part of TR that relates to building skills and increasing employees' market value.

Importance of Justice, Dignity, and Respect:

TR from a biblical viewpoint upholds the values of justice, dignity, and respect integral to any successful HRM. Leviticus 19:13 (KJV) insists, "Thou shalt not defraud thy neighbour, neither rob him: the wages of him that is hired shall not abide with thee all night until the morning." Total rewards must be distributed fairly with dignity and respect, without any bias or favoritism.

Adopting a biblical perspective to the contemporary Total Rewards System in HRM allows for a holistic and ethical approach to employee benefits and compensation. The parables and teachings relay principles in favor of equity, compassion, and investment in personal growth, adding depth and wider significance to the strategic distribution of rewards. This involves integrating both tangible and intangible rewards that resonate with biblical teachings of justice, fairness, and respect for the dignity of labor. These set the stage for a more compassionate, empathetic, and efficient total rewards system that goes beyond the transactional relationship between an employer and employee.

The relevance of biblical perspectives in shaping the landscape of strategic HRM serves as a reminder that despite technological and economic advancements of the 21st-century, foundational principles of fairness, generosity, and respect remain timeless and universal in ensuring the successful management of human resources

Chapter 10: Employee Relations in Contemporary SHRM

The ever-changing dynamics within the 21st-century workplace underscore the imperative need for an effective strategic approach to employee relations. Modern businesses operate within a progressive and increasingly complex environment where employee engagement, motivation, and satisfaction become instrumental in driving overall organizational performance. Effective management of employee relations has thus evolved as a central piece in the strategic HRM puzzle where the key focus has shifted from the traditional 'command and control' model to a more participant-oriented approach.

In the last two decades, significant changes in the global economic environment, dynamic technological advances, and generational shifts in employees' attitudes and expectations have posed new challenges and opportunities for managing employee relations. While these trends carry significant implications for SHRM, they also call for new methodologies that can address the growing complexities associated with managing diverse, multi-generational workforces in an increasingly digitalized world.

A good SHRM approach to employee relations in the 21st Century aims toward creating a supportive work environment where employees can thrive and maximize their potential, and where their contributions are recognized and valued. It includes strategies that foster open communication, encourage worker participation in decision-making, maintain fair compensation and benefit systems, and promote opportunities for learning and development.

Firstly, management transparency and open communication have become critical to fostering trust within the organization. SHRM leverages multiple channels of communication, including digital platforms, to ensure information transparency and encourage dialogue between employees and management. Such an approach not only makes employees feel valued but also increases their understanding of business operations and their roles, which in turn aids efficiency and productivity.

Secondly, employee participation in decision-making is emphasized as it instills a sense of ownership and responsibility among employees, ultimately enhancing their commitment to organizational goals. Strategies like implementing suggestion boxes or rotating leadership are a few examples that have proved efficacious in the past.

Next, establishing equitable compensation and benefits regimes is an indispensable part of a robust SHRM approach. HR professionals carefully devise and implement remuneration policies that fairly reward employees' efforts and maintain internal equity and external competitiveness. This strategy ensures the retention of high-performing employees and helps attract capable talent.

Lastly, prospects for learning and development are prominent in enhancing employee satisfaction and motivation. Progressive businesses now invest heavily in rendering their staff with opportunities for growth, learning, and advancement as an integral part of their strategic HRM.

In the current, rapidly evolving business landscape, successful SHRM necessitates not only aligning employee relations strategies with the organization's strategic goals but also fostering a culture of collaboration, fairness, and continuous learning. Forward-thinking HRM will no doubt continue to adapt and innovate, ensuring they remain equipped to navigate the complexities of 21st-century employee relations.

Essentially, in the twenty-first century, employee relations encompass much more than merely enforcing workplace policies. It involves strategically managing the workplace environment to foster symbiotic relationships between employees and employers. In essence, it is all about capitalizing on human capabilities in the journey towards organizational excellence.

Navigating Employee Relations: A Case Study

The Big Tech Corporation is a leading firm in the technology sector, boasting over 10,000 employees globally. This case study explores contemporary practices in strategic human resource management (SHRM) that Big Tech Corporation has implemented to manage employee relations, with particular emphasis on the role of communication, negotiation, and conflict resolution.

The Challenge

In 2018, Big Tech Corporation faced a crescendo of employee dissatisfaction, culminating in low morale, high turnover, and a public relations nightmare as disgruntled employees voiced their concerns in the media. The HR team recognized the need for strategic, comprehensive measures to rebuild trust, enhance communication, and foster a more inclusive corporate culture.

SHRM Interventions:

A. **Enhanced Communication Channels**: Big Tech Corporation revamped their existing hierarchical communication system. They introduced an open-door policy, allowing employees at all levels to communicate matters directly with management, without fear of retaliation.

B. **A Central Negotiation Platform**: The corporation created an online platform where employees can express their collective concerns, submit proposals for change, or negotiate terms directly with the HR team. This platform allows for greater transparency and constructive negotiation.

C. **Conflict Resolution Training**: The management staff were trained in conflict resolution techniques. Mediation units were instituted department-wise to address conflicts at the grassroots level.

Evaluation of Outcomes

Since the implementation of these SHRM measures, employee satisfaction as per annual surveys has seen substantial improvement, and the attrition rate has fallen by approximately 20%. The open-door policy fostered a climate of trust and transparency, leading to a significant reduction in issues escalated to higher management. The central negotiation platform played a pivotal role in addressing collective grievances, improving workplace relations, and giving birth to new company policies.

Lessons Learned

The Big Tech Corporation's experience vividly illustrates that effective employee relations management is at the heart of an organization's success. Strategic implementation of robust communication channels, innovative negotiation platforms, and effective conflict resolution mechanisms contribute to a healthy working environment, leading to happier, more productive employees.

Conclusion

Effective strategic human resource management practices that focus on enhanced employee relations not only improve morale and productivity but also play a vital role in shaping positive organizational culture. Organizations, such as Big Tech Corporation, that prioritize employee engagement and satisfaction reap the rewards in the form of loyalty, better performance, and a more positive public image. In conclusion, robust employee relations are the cornerstone of every successful enterprise. By incorporating SHRM interventions aimed at managing and enhancing employee relations, businesses can set themselves up for long-term success.

Employee Relations from a Biblical Perspective in Contemporary SHRM

An efficient HR strategy acknowledges the fluidity of today's fast-paced, global marketplace and is open-minded about contemporary perspectives. From a Biblical standpoint, the essential themes remain consistent: ethical behaviors, compassion, justice, kindness, and respect—the foundational pillars of exemplary employee relations.

The 21st Century Human Resources Management (HRM) goes beyond mere business transactions; it encompasses the organization's heart and soul, which is its people. The benchmark perspective resonates through the Biblical scripture found in Proverbs 16:11 (KJV) implies fairness and justice, two key imperatives in modern employee relations. Also, in Leviticus 19:13 (KJV), the principle of fair compensation is underscored. This scripture articulates that employers must pay employees their due compensation on time.

Further, Ephesians 4:2-3(KJV) exalts humility, patience, and tolerance in maintaining unity—timeless advice for employers to foster a harmonious and inclusive workplace environment. The golden rule outlined in Luke 6:31 (KJV) spells out the basis of respect and consideration that should govern relations between employers and employees and between co-workers. Such Biblical maxims assist in devising HR strategies that promote respect, tolerance, inclusivity, and cohesion, thus thankfully steering away from the depersonalized view of employees as mere workforce.

The Bible's teachings regarding work ethics, specifically diligence and integrity, are directly applicable to the modern workplace. Colossians 3:23–24, for instance, inspires employees to work diligently with integrity: " And whatsoever ye do, do it heartily, as to the Lord, and not unto men; knowing that of the Lord ye shall receive the reward of the inheritance: for ye serve the Lord Christ." These verses are a compelling reminder for employees to maintain high levels of professionalism and commitment, as their work is not just a service to their employer, but ultimately to God.

Lastly, it is important to note that while the Bible offers valuable insights for employee relations, HR strategies must also align with legal frameworks, and respect cultural and religious diversity in the 21st Century workplace. Therefore, applying a Biblical perspective on employee relations requires wisdom to balance these scriptures with contemporary HRM tools and strategies to establish and uphold fairness, respect, inclusivity, and dignity in the workplace.

Overall, from a Biblical perspective, the 21st century HRM must prioritize just and equitable treatment of employees, fair pay, workplace efficiency, and a community-oriented environment to cultivate meaningful relationships and interactions. As these traditional values echoed from Biblical times find universal acceptance in modern times, they are to didactically act as the guiding principles in shaping the strategic HRM policies and to lead to fruitful and sustainable employee relations.

Chapter 11: Employee Engagement in Contemporary SHRM

Employee engagement is a crucial factor in the modern framework of Strategic Human Resource Management (SHRM). With rising competition, increased diversity, and the ever-changing face of the business ecosystem, an engaged workforce forms the core foundation enabling organizational success.

In the recent era, employee engagement has transcended from being just a 'feel-good' factor to a strategic driver of organizational efficiency and effectiveness. Contemporary SHRM recognizes this and focuses on nurturing a work environment that promotes active engagement, thereby enhancing overall performance and productivity.

An engaged workforce is typically characterized by higher job satisfaction, stronger commitment, and superior job performance. These employees are passionate about their work and display a high level of professional involvement, going above and beyond their job duties and contributing significantly to the company's goals. By fostering engagement, organizations can reduce turnover rates and improve retention, thus leading to cost-saving benefits.

Contemporary SHRM strides towards emphasizing employee engagement via initiatives like competency-based job designs, reward systems, and talent management programs. These practices not only stimulate the employees to perform at their best, but also foster effective communication, promote creativity, and create a sustainable work culture.

Furthermore, in a changing business landscape where remote work and digital collaboration are increasingly common, engagement strategies may need to evolve to consider these new paradigms. Contemporary SHRM approaches should consider these changes, offering flexible work arrangements and using technology to promote interaction and collaboration.

Generally, the role of employee engagement in contemporary SHRM cannot be overemphasized. To thrive in a competitive environment, businesses must prioritize cultivating an engaged workforce, as its benefits directly influence the bottom line and long-term organizational growth. Initiatives to promote engagement can help employees become more aligned with the business's mission, vision, and goals, consequently improving the overall organizational climate.

As an HR consultant, my recommendation to businesses would be to invest time and resources in developing effective employee engagement strategies that align with the company's overall strategic objectives. This would ensure not just a competent workforce, but a profitable enterprise built on the pillars of engagement, satisfaction, and high performance.

Employee Engagement in Contemporary SHRM: A Case Study

In the dynamic business landscape of the 21st century, there lived a concept that had changed drastically over time yet was significant in its relevance and criticality - Employee Engagement. This concept, influenced by profound strategic thinking and refinements, transitioned from a term often tossed around in corporate boardrooms to a powerful strategic tool in the Human Resources arsenal.

Once considered a mere tick mark in the list of HR responsibilities, Employee Engagement underwent a significant evolution. From being about event planning and team outings, it metamorphosed into a strategic approach for businesses aiming to heighten productivity, retain talent, and improve the quality of work life. Its importance in the corporate world was further heightened due to complex factors such as globalization, innovations in technology, changing demographics and psychographics, and the increasing trend of remote work - everything that defines the 21st-century corporate panorama.

In the city of Strategica, a company named Winning Inc was grappling to control employee turnover, facing a consistent dip in productivity, and witnessing a gradual decline in the level of job satisfaction among employees. The HR head, Captain Engage, after a comprehensive study and analysis, perceived that the root cause of all these issues was low employee engagement. He decided to shape a new age strategy to enhance engagement levels, integrating it with the broader HR and business strategy.

Captain Engage initiated surveys to understand the pulse of the organization. This backed by sound analytics, helped him identify the pain points and gaps in the current scenario. The findings suggested that employees had started viewing their work as just a means to earn their livelihood, instead of being a source of satisfaction and growth. The poor work-life balance and lack of recognition were disengaging them, affecting their overall performance.

To combat this problem, Captain Engage embraced flexibility and introduced a host of work-from-home, flexible working hours, and part-time working schemes. This was aimed at promoting a healthier work-life balance and accommodating the individual needs of employees. Next, he integrated recognition into every aspect of the company culture. He introduced a peer-to-peer recognition platform, encouraging employees to appreciate each other's efforts and achievements.

Simultaneously, Winning Inc under the guidance of the Captain developed mentorship programs and continuous learning opportunities, that would help employees grow, both personally and professionally. The organization's culture was transformed into one that celebrates progress and encourages feedback. This led to employees feeling valued, respected, and more engaged.

In a matter of months, Winning Inc began to witness a notable positive shift. The employee turnover rate considerably dipped, and productivity made friends with heights like never before. The job satisfaction score mirrored this success story boasting record-high figures. It was quite evident that Employee engagement had worked its strategic magic yet again.

The story of Winning Inc is not merely emulative but a manifestation of HR's capacity and strategic capability in engaging employees. Employee Engagement in the 21st century is not just about fun at work. Rather, it is about fostering a work environment that motivates employees, improves their job satisfaction, promotes their well-being, and hence, optimally leads to the achievement of organizational objectives. This strategic approach not only helps retain the best talent but also elevates the overall growth and success of the organization.

Employee Engagement in Contemporary SHRM: A Biblical Perspective

In contemporary SHRM, the concept of employee engagement has grown progressively popular and vital to creating a thriving, productive work environment. Interestingly, the Bible provides timeless principles that are incredibly applicable when analyzing this concept, even in our digitized, globalized 21st-century context.

Starting from the biblical context, Colossians 3:23 (KJV) counsels, "whatsoever ye do, do it heartily, as to the Lord, and not unto men." Individual engagement at the workplace not only contributes positively to the overall strategic objectives but is depicted as an act of reverence towards God. In essence, this principle from the Bible exhorts employees to be industrious, dedicated, and loyal because their ultimate accountability lies with God, not just their human supervisors.

From an HRM standpoint, the principle stresses the significance of intrinsic motivation: the manifesto that propels employees to work productively and meaningfully. It highlights the need for fostering conditions that inspire employees to give their best, viewing their job as a calling rather than just a means to an end. Relevant initiatives might include fostering work environments that encourage individual growth, offering emotionally gratifying roles, and providing fair compensation.

Another insightful verse is Proverbs 27:17 (KJV). The essence of this wisdom text emphasizes teamwork and interdependence among employees, an essential factor in bolstering employee engagement. It speaks to the necessity of creating a corporate culture founded on mutual respect, camaraderie, and cooperation. Building such an environment enhances job satisfaction and reinforces a sense of belonging, a crucial tool in fueling employee engagement.

In the same line, the biblical principle of servant leadership drawn from Mark 10:43-45

(KJV) encourages leaders to serve their followers rather than lord it over them. In a modern HRM setup, this leadership model can significantly heighten employee engagement. When lived out in the workplace, it fosters mutual respect between management and employees, thereby creating an environment that encourages active engagement.

The 21st century has observed companies switch to employee-centric approaches. Luke 6:31 (KJV) is a timeless gem that reinforces this shift. It advocates for the dignified, fair, and respectful treatment of all employees –a powerful catalyst in encouraging employee participation and enthusiasm.

The Bible, while ancient, offers valuable wisdom that modern HR professionals can apply to foster employee engagement. The ultimate goal remains the same: to create an environment where employees can thrive, both individually and collectively, in their bid to achieve strategic organizational objectives. Implementing these biblical principles will not only cultivate a culture of employee engagement but also foster a holistically successful and robust organization.

Chapter 12: Diversity Management in Contemporary SHRM

In the constantly evolving business landscape, the importance of diversity and inclusion in SHRM cannot be overemphasized. Contemporary businesses increasingly recognize that a diverse and inclusive workforce brings broader perspectives, promotes innovation, improves decision-making, enriches organizational culture, and enhances overall business performance.

Diversity extends beyond merely the legally protected categories (such as gender, race, and age) to include diversity of thought, experiences, backgrounds, and skills. A diverse workforce affords organizations a competitive advantage in today's global marketplace. It allows for greater creativity and innovation, leading to better problem-solving capabilities. Different individuals bring different perspectives into play, offering richer insights into market trends, customer behavior, and business strategies.

Meanwhile, inclusion is about cultivating an environment where all employees feel valued, included, and empowered to contribute their best. It's not enough just to have a diverse team; the organization also must create an environment that allows every member to contribute fully. A truly inclusive environment promotes open communication, respects diverse views, and encourages participation.

In modern SHRM, the objective of diversity and inclusion initiatives is not only about meeting legal requirements or presenting a positive image but also about leveraging diversity and inclusion for strategic advantages. This means integrating diversity and inclusion into strategic HRM processes, from recruitment and selection, training and development to performance management and reward systems.

Recruitment and selection processes are critical to building a diverse workforce. Human resource practitioners must ensure that job advertisements, screenings, and interviews do not discriminate against any group. Taking diversity into account in training and development ensures that employees develop competencies to work effectively in diverse environments. Performance management systems should recognize and reward not just business outcomes but also behaviors promoting diversity and inclusion.

While implementing diversity and inclusion initiatives, businesses should be mindful of possible challenges. The benefits of diversity can easily be undermined by conscious or unconscious biases, discrimination, or antisocial behaviors. Therefore, businesses need to promote a culture that values diversity and takes a firm stance against any form of discrimination.

Overall, in the contemporary business environment, diversity and inclusion should be key considerations in strategic HRM. Rather than being seen as stand-alone programs or initiatives, they should be integrated into each aspect of human resource practices and strategies. By doing this, businesses can utilize the full potential of their diverse workforce and foster a culture of inclusion, leading to improved organizational performance and competitive advantage.

Diversity and Inclusion in Contemporary SHRM: A Case Study

In the city of Megapolis, a dynamic tech company named BlueTech was grappling with an unidentified stumbling block in its path toward global market dominance. The company was rich with advanced technology, exceptional talents, and valuable stakeholders. Despite these resources and potential, BlueTech struggled to harness creative solutions and new perspectives, which were imperative to sustaining competitive advantage in the 21st century's dynamic business environment.

In response, BlueTech hired an HR consultant, Natalie Hurd, an expert specializing in strategic human resources management. Upon arrival, Hurd quickly identified the flaw in BlueTech's armor - lack of diversity and inclusion.

Diversity, as Hurd explained to the BlueTech management team, was not just an ethical imperative or a corporate social responsibility, but a strategic advantage in the modern world. She echoed the 21st-century mantra of HR management - a diverse workforce equates to diverse ideas, thoughts, and service capabilities.

BlueTech's existing structure was heavily homogeneous, with similar backgrounds, ethnicities, and career paths dominating the workforce lineup. Hurd posited this lack of diversity had caused a dearth of innovation, creativity, and ultimately competitiveness for BlueTech.

To address this, Hurd drew the BlueTech roadmap towards establishing a more diverse and inclusive workforce. She emphasized addressing cognitive biases such as affinity bias and confirmation bias during the hiring process. She suggested BlueTech explore historically black colleges and universities, women's colleges, and similar institutions to ensure the hiring pipeline was richly diverse.

Diversity, though, was not enough. Hurd addressed the other critical part of the equation — inclusion. Unless BlueTech's diverse employees felt valued, recognized, and included, their unique perspectives couldn't better the team's decision-making or innovation capabilities. For that, she laid out several strategic plans for fostering an inclusive atmosphere. These involved manager training programs to recognize unconscious bias, promote a culture of respect and acceptance, and implement effective communication channels.

Over time, these changes brought about an extraordinary transformation. BlueTech's transformed workforce became an amalgamation of various cultures, experiences, and viewpoints. Their deliberations became more inclusive, and their solutions more innovative. BlueTech began breaking its previous performance records, venturing successfully into uncharted territories.

When the dust settled, BlueTech stood as an exemplar of diversity and inclusion in strategic HR management, illustrating the relevance and necessity of these constructs in the modern corporate arena. They proved that investing in diversity and fostering inclusion was not an expensive compliance obligation but a lucrative strategic investment.

Remarkably, in the contemporary 21st-century business environment, diversity and inclusion have moved on from being just buzzwords to an integral part of strategic HR management. It is no longer a trend, but an essential, interwoven component of business strategy, driving innovation, workplace culture, brand reputation, customer relationship, and ultimately, business success. They have emerged as potential game-changers in the volatile, uncertain, complex, and ambiguous times that we navigate today.

BlueTech's transformational journey from being a homogeneous tech company to a prosperous diverse powerhouse underlines the strategic importance of diversity and inclusion. It illustrates that diversity and inclusion are not merely moral imperatives but compelling business strategies critical to survival, competitiveness, and growth in the 21st century.

Diversity and Inclusion in Contemporary SHRM: A Biblical Perspective

Evolving in a globally connected society, modern-day organizations are going through a major transformation. Human Resources Management (HRM) is embracing diversity and inclusion to foster a harmonious work environment conducive to innovation and growth. This shift aligns with biblical virtues, which stress the significance of mutual respect, equality, and love for all, regardless of one's race, culture, or socio-economic standing.

The Bible, in Galatians 3:28 (KJV), implicitly underlines the essence of diversity and inclusion, pushing for an egalitarian society where identity is not confined to superficial determinants but bonded by love and unity.

In 1 Corinthians 12 (KJV), Apostle Paul writes about the diversity of the parts of the body and their interdependence. He points out that every part has a unique role, contributing to the overall functioning of the body. When one part is in pain so is the entire body, and when one part is honored, so is the entire body. The metaphor translates well to HRM, highlighting that regardless of individual roles, each employee forms an integral part of the organization. HR must ensure inclusivity in that every employee's unique skill set, background, and perspectives are valued, setting a path for shared success.

The Book of Acts narrates the story of Pentecost, which symbolizes the birth of the first multi-ethnic, cross-cultural church. The Holy Spirit enabled the disciples to speak in various languages, ensuring the gospel message was accessible to all, irrespective of linguistic differences. This is a powerful testament to rebuking exclusivity and embracing diversity. It sets a mandate for HRs to eliminate prejudiced practices and develop multilingual, multicultural workplaces, contributing to enriched creativity and broader viewpoints.

The biblical tale of the Good Samaritan narrates the act of a Samaritan man helping an injured Jew, showcasing compassion towards a fellow human being without bias of nationality or religion. It sends a strong message of empathy for HR managers, who should foster a culture of respect and acceptance, not merely tolerance, amongst organizational members.

The 21st-century SHRM, with its priorities set on diversity and inclusion, mirrors these biblical perspectives. Biblical teachings impart ethical guidance, fostering a more empathetic, accepting corporate culture. Companies that employ biblical concepts of diversity and inclusion can anticipate richer innovation, enhanced employee engagement and productivity, improved problem-solving and decision-making capacities, and increased competitive advantage.

As HR consultants, our mission and vision should align with these integral values, advocating for diverse human capital and inclusive organizational practices that respect the dignity of every individual. Let us remember Proverbs 22:2: "The rich and poor meet together: the Lord is the maker of them all." This verse serves as a reminder that every individual is equal and valuable to God, and hence, should be given equal opportunity and respect in the workplace.

Corporates' quest for sustenance and progression is not solely economic but extends to the broader societal contribution. It is in embracing diversity and fostering a culturally diverse and inclusive work environment that organizations, helped by HR strategically enforced practices, can evolve truly, and fulfill their broader commitments.

Chapter 13: Enhancing Employee Wellbeing, Work-Life-Balance, and Health in 21st Century SHRM

The role of Human Resources (HR) has evolved significantly in the 21st Century, moving far beyond traditional administrative and compliance functions. Nowadays, HR departments play a strategic role in creating a culture that motivates employees, nurtures their potential, and maximizes their productivity. One of the critical areas in this strategic approach is focusing on employee wellbeing, work-life balance, and health.

Importance of Employee Wellbeing

A strong focus on employee well-being leads to enhanced job satisfaction, heightened morale, and increased overall performance. Employees operating at their best can significantly boost the overall productivity of the organization, thus positively influencing the bottom line. In this regard, strategic HRM should implement structures that cater to employees' wellbeing, such as offering a healthy work environment, offering psychological support or counseling, promoting a nurturing company culture, and encouraging team-building activities.

Understanding Work-Life Balance

The ever-evolving dynamic of the working environment in the 21st Century, especially with the rise of remote work, necessitates a redefined approach to work-life balance. As a strategic HR consultant, it becomes critical to create guidelines that allow employees to balance their personal life commitments and work obligations effectively. Providing flexible work schedules, advocating for time off, and remote and part-time work options are strategies that can enhance work-life balance. Positive work-life balance results in reduced burnout and turnover rates, translating to increased productivity and overall improved organizational performance.

Investing in Health in the Workplace

Employee health and wellness are critical considerations in 21st-century strategic HR management. A healthy employee is a productive employee. Corporations can actively participate in promoting employee health through the initiation of wellness programs that encourage regular exercise, providing healthy meals or snacks, and regular health check-ups. Mental health is also an integral part of overall health, and initiatives like counseling services, stress management workshops, and mental health days off greatly contribute to mental well-being. Ensuring a healthy work environment, both physically and psychologically, also reduces health-related absences and promotes team cohesion and motivation.

Overall, a 21st-century SHRM approach places a strong emphasis on employee well-being, work-life balance, and health. By integrating these areas into the core HR functions, organizations can create a nurturing and motivated workforce, ready to meet the demands of the contemporary business environment and the ever-evolving workplace norms. HR should, therefore, take the lead in initiating policies and developing a culture that promotes employee wellbeing, work-life balance, and health and ensuring they are not merely boxes to check, but integrated into the very fabric of the organization.

Enhancing Employee Wellbeing, Work-Life-Balance, and Health in 21st Century SHRM: AstraTech Case

This case study unravels the relationship between these factors and their significance in boosting organizational productivity, loyalty, and overall performance in the 21st century. The corporation under study is AstraTech, a notable tech industry leader with over 10,000 employees globally.

AstraTech experienced consistent growth for five years until it hit a roadblock in 2019, resulting in a 22% rise in employee turnover and a 15% dip in performance metrics. Independent audits revealed that these bottlenecks were driven by employee health issues, amplified stress levels, and poor work-life balance. These findings necessitated changes to AstraTech's strategic HRM approach.

AstraTech's HRM responded by implementing several strategic initiatives aimed at fostering a culture of wellness, promoting better work-life balance, and improving employees' overall health.

- **Wellness Programs and Policies** - Comprising of fitness challenges, mental health awareness drives, and provisions for counseling sessions. They pursued 'positive psychology' where the focus moved from 'fixing what's wrong' to 'building what's right' with the employees.

- **Flexible Work Arrangements**- Employees were given the option to work from home, opt for flexible timings, and use 'unlimited vacations', recognizing the need for time off to balance personal and professional commitments.
- **Healthcare initiatives**- Partnered with healthcare service providers for regular health check-ups and wellness sessions to monitor, report, and address health concerns of their workforce.

After a year of these changes, AstraTech noticed a significant improvement in the key areas that were originally underperforming.

- **Employee turnover** dropped by 12%, and performance metrics shot up by 20%.
- The **Rate of Absenteeism** plummeted, while both employee engagement and overall job satisfaction scores saw substantial boosts.
- **Productivity** hit a three-year high, with reports of increased innovation and problem-solving abilities among work teams.

These indicators were not only encouraging but also corroborative of the growing body of research underscoring the importance of employee well-being in 21st-century workplaces.

This case manifests the critical need for SHRM to incorporate employee well-being, work-life balance, and health in their operational framework. AstraTech's early missteps and subsequent recovery underscore the fact that neglecting these facets can have significant repercussions on organizational performance while paying heed can yield substantial gains.

As the 21st-century corporate landscape evolves, these components have become integral and unavoidable elements of strategic HRM – ensuring not just the progression of their employees, but the overall success of the organization in a highly competitive business space.

A Biblical Perspective on Employee Well-being, Work-Life Balance, and Health in Contemporary SHRM

In our ever-evolving 21st-century workplace, SHRM plays a critical role in fostering employee well-being, work-life balance, and health. There is a profound connection between these elements and productivity. This dialogue maps this practice to the principles laid out in the Bible, demonstrating the inherent timelessness of these values and principles in promoting a robust workforce.

Employee Well-being: Proverbs 16:24 (KJV) articulates, "Pleasant words are as an honeycomb, sweet to the soul, and health to the bones." This emphasizes the power of kind words in fostering a positive work atmosphere which in turn promotes overall well-being. In strategic HRM, this principle translates into strong interpersonal communication, constructive feedback, and accolades for a job well-done. Policies reflecting preventive healthcare, and mental health support in the form of counseling, wellness programs, and recreational activities can maintain and enhance the employee's well-being.

Work-Life Balance: Exodus 20:8-10 (KJV) binds us to "Remember the sabbath day, to keep it holy. Six days shalt thou labour, and do all thy work: But the seventh day is the sabbath of the Lord thy God: in it, thou shalt not do any work, thou, nor thy son, nor thy daughter, thy manservant, nor thy maidservant, nor thy cattle, nor thy stranger that is within thy gates:" This principle instills the necessity of maintaining a balance between work and rest. In contemporary HRM, these values align with fostering work-life balance via flexible work hours, remote work possibilities, encouraging employees to take time off, etc., reducing employee burnout and leading to increased satisfaction and productivity.

Employee Health: 3 John 1:2 states, "Beloved, I wish above all things that thou mayest prosper and be in health, even as thy soul prospereth."

While considering the Biblical perspective on employee health, it is essential to note this verse which directly points to the importance of maintaining good health. Today's HRM activities should focus on promoting a healthy workplace, which involves safe working conditions, comprehensive insurance coverage, regular health check-ups, ergonomic workstations, and more.

Contemporary SHRM, navigating the challenges of the 21st century, must align more with these timeless biblical values. Organizations that lean on these principles represent a haven in which employees can thrive. They create a culture that nurtures well-being, facilitates work-life balance, promotes health, and consequently, boosts productivity. Therefore, fostering an environment based on Biblical perspectives will undoubtedly yield positive outcomes for organizations in our modern workspace.

I hope that this perspective encourages reflection on your HR policies and stimulates ideas on using these principles as a roadmap to a more empathetic and resilient workforce.

Chapter 14: Change Management in Contemporary SHRM

Change Management, a critical component of strategic human resources management, has evolved significantly in the contemporary 21st-century business environment. As organizations operate in an increasingly dynamic, technologically driven, and global context, Change Management arises as a responsible endeavor to tackle these complexities while ensuring a smooth transition for employees, business processes, culture, and the organization's overall system.

The primary objective of Change Management within SHRM is to systematically address change and its impact on organizations and their employees from a strategic standpoint. As an essential element of strategic planning, Change Management invariably drives business success by aligning workforce capabilities with organizational goals.

Today, Change Management is no longer confined to a procedural aspect of business; instead, it is viewed as an organizational culture and a mindset wherein adaptability, flexibility, and resilience are embedded in the business DNA. It includes employee engagement, leadership alignment, effective communication, and adequate training and development.

The role of Change Management within SHRM has intensified due to enforceable factors like globalization, technological advancements, diversity, and evolving job roles. Additionally, organizations are compelled to respond to regulatory changes, consumer demands, and market competition. Consequently, strategic HRM, coupled with Change Management, is indispensable for fostering organizational readiness, building resilience, and ensuring business continuity.

In the face of technological disruption, there's an evident shift towards digital HRM - a testament to the current transformation within SHRM. Automation, Artificial Intelligence, and analytics are redefining job roles and HR processes, demanding organizations to adopt these changes to thrive. HR professionals are not just the facilitators of this transition, but they also need to equip themselves with these new-age skills.

As the workforce demographics diversify, Change Management helps organizations to foster inclusivity. It facilitates multicultural dexterity and establishes protocols to manage generational, gender, cultural and linguistic differences within the workforce. Thus, inclusivity becomes a strategic imperative for organizational success in today's hyperconnected world.

All of this underscores the need for change-ready leadership. Leaders must possess the ability to navigate their teams through change while mitigating resistance, fostering engagement, and instilling confidence and commitment. In this regard, HR is instrumental in coaching leaders to practice empathy, emotional intelligence, and resilience.

Overall, Change Management in contemporary 21st-century SHRM is an ongoing, proactive process needed to adapt, survive, and thrive in the face of change. It necessitates strategic alignment, leadership engagement, technological adoption, and inclusive practices. As HR Consultants, it's crucial to evolve in our roles as change advocates and facilitators, driving businesses forward and around obstacles in their path to success.

Change Management in Contemporary SHRM: XYZ Corporation Case

XYZ Corporation is a well-established multinational technology firm, operating in 25 countries with approximately 50,000 employees.

The company embarked on a substantial reorganization - modernizing its business structure through digitization and agility to better serve its client base, compete with emerging tech startups, and adapt to the rapid pace of technological innovation. Central to this transformational quest was a strategic shift in the company's approach to Human Resources Management.

    The reorganization eventually demanded changes in job roles, restructuring of teams, implementation of new methodologies, and the introduction of cutting-edge technologies. This overhaul led to widespread resistance amongst personnel due to apprehension of job security, lack of digital skills, and fear of adjusting to new operating models. The challenge posed for the HR team was to initiate an effective change management strategy to overcome employee resistance and transition smoothly into the new organizational design.

The HR team recognized the gravity of the situation and adhered to three significant principles of strategic HR management in the change process: communication, training, and participation.

Communication: A clear, detailed, and timely communication strategy was employed. HR defined the consequences of not changing, strategic objectives, and potential benefits of the transformation. They enabled an open-door policy for employee queries and concerns which helped to decrease uncertainty and anxieties.

Training: Recognizing that new skills were indispensable for digitization, XYZ Corporation set up training programs to equip employees with the necessary expertise, thereby reducing their fear of becoming irrelevant in the digital age.

Employee Participation: HR included employees in the decision-making process, hence reducing resistance and increasing acceptance of the change. Employee feedback was incorporated where feasible, thereby encouraging a sense of ownership among staff.

The strategic HR interventions resulted in a gradual decrease in resistance to change. Employees began demonstrating a willingness to adapt to the upgraded business model, showcasing enhanced productivity and efficiency. A marked improvement in employee morale and job satisfaction was also observed, contributing to a healthier work environment.

This case conclusively demonstrates the critical role of strategic human resource management in successful change management. A thoughtful and inclusive approach can effectively reduce resistance and encourage acceptance of change. Companies implementing substantial changes should therefore invest in empowering their HR teams, by allocating resources and training to aid in managing change. HR practices should remain flexible and adapt to the evolving needs of employees throughout the change management process.

This case study exemplifies that embracing change rather than resisting, is the key to surviving in the rapidly transforming world of 21st century business. It underlines the necessity of effective HR strategic management, placing it at the forefront of successful business transformations.

As we are well into the 21st century, with the world evolving faster than ever before, this case study offers valuable insights into how the modern HR professional can navigate the complex dynamics of change in the contemporary business environment. It demonstrates that the principles of communication, training, and participation remain timeless, providing a solid foundation upon which to build a successful, progressive organization that is ready to meet the challenges of the future.

Change Management in Contemporary SHRM: A Biblical Perspective

Understanding change management from a biblical perspective illuminates the enduring principles and values that can guide contemporary strategic human resource management. Various biblical narratives underline the inevitability of change and the importance of adapting strategically to shifting circumstances. From these, we can glean valuable insights into managing change effectively in the 21st-century business environment, grounded in timeless truths.

In Proverbs 24:6 (KJV), it is stated, "For by wise counsel thou shalt make thy war: and in multitude of counsellors there is safety." This verse gives credence to the strategic aspect of change management. It emphasizes the necessity of informed, educated advice for successful outcomes. The strategic human resource manager, therefore, needs to engage wisdom, broad knowledge, and diverse opinions to navigate change successfully.

This wisdom begins with the understanding that change is inevitable. Ecclesiastes 3:1 (KJV) insists "To every thing there is a season, and a time to every purpose under the heaven." This timeless wisdom can be translated to mean that change is constant and must be managed proactively. Organizations must create an environment conducive to change, where employees understand its necessity, and can adapt swiftly.

The principle of servant leadership, embodied by Christ Himself (Mark 10:45, KJV), is another critical biblical perspective relevant to strategic HR management. It fosters a culture of mutual respect, engagement, and empowerment – keys to successful change management. By putting others' needs first and helping people develop and perform as highly as possible, HR leaders can help employees navigate the trepidation often associated with change, hence cultivating a supportive atmosphere that fosters successful change implementation.

Additionally, the value of integrity and honesty embedded in the biblical teachings (Proverbs 10:9, KJV) should be at the heart of change management strategies. Transparency in communicating the why, how, and what of change initiatives is key to gaining employee trust and commitment. Honest communication minimizes resistance to change and creates a sense of shared ownership and accountability.

The notion of grace and forgiveness, stressed throughout the New Testament, also plays a critical role in change management. It's essential to create a safe environment where learning from mistakes is encouraged and not penalized. Such a grace-filled atmosphere fosters innovation, a catalyst of organizational adaptation to change.

Applying biblical principles to change management lends to effective guidance in 21st-century SHRM. Recognizing change as a constant, seeking wisdom in guidance, embracing servant leadership, fostering integrity, and extending grace encapsulate a biblically-based approach to change management. This approach, when applied effectively, has the potential to cultivate resilient organizations that embrace change as an integral part of growth and innovation.

These principles are timeless and offer a perspective on change management in HR – one that goes beyond traditional business strategy and incorporates values that foster mutual respect, integrity, and growth for all stakeholders involved.

Chapter 15: Compliance & Risk Management in Contemporary SHRM

Amidst constant changes in the technological forefront, global geopolitics, and social dynamics, it is crucial that human resource professionals not only positively interact with these changes but also lead, predict, and manage future organizational trajectories. Increasingly, two aspects have gained prominence in SHRM: compliance and risk management.

Effective compliance encompasses an adherence to a plethora of regulations and policies including labor laws, compensation and benefits requirements, employee rights provisions, safety mandates, and ethical standards, among others. In an age where information is easily accessible and transparency is demanded, non-compliance can cause severe repercussions, including legal penalties, reputation damage, and decreased employee morale. Therefore, HR professionals need to ensure an organizational culture that recognizes and emphasizes the importance of compliance.

In doing so, a two-tier approach is beneficial: top-down and bottom-up. A top-down approach reflects implementing compliance strategies and regulations at the top management level, which then trickles down to all hierarchical levels of the organization. The bottom-up approach, on the other hand, involves educating and engaging employees at all levels, creating a shared sense of responsibility toward compliance.

Risk Management is another crucial aspect of SHRM that pertains to the detection, evaluation, and mitigation of potential risks associated with managing human resources. These risks may arise from various sources such as talent management, workforce diversity, leadership succession, competitive environments, and even global crises such as the COVID-19 pandemic.

The process of risk management entails three stages: identification, analysis, and treatment. Risk identification involves understanding potential threats, followed by risk analysis, which evaluates these risks' nature, scope, and potential impact. Lastly, risk treatment includes deciding and implementing measures to control or mitigate the risks.

However, it is worth noting that in today's volatile business environment, risk is not necessarily a threat but can represent an opportunity. Therefore, a "proactive" risk management strategy, which involves predicting and preparing for future risks, can provide a competitive edge by turning risks into strategic opportunities.

To conclude, incorporating compliance and risk management into SHRM in the 21st century ensures not just the survival but the growth and development of an organization. Furthermore, by fostering a culture of compliance and proactive risk management within the organization, HR professionals can enhance operational efficiency, build a strong company reputation, and establish a resilient organization.

Compliance & Risk Management in Contemporary SHRM: MBTech Case

This case study explores the implications of compliance and risk management in strategic HRM within MBTech, a global technology firm. MBTech, a multinational technology firm, experienced rapid growth over the past five years, expanding to more than 15 countries. It managed to approach HR practices relatively loosely, often customized to individual or regional team preferences. However, as the organization scaled, inconsistencies and irregularities in HR operations emerged, leaving MBTech vulnerable to compliance-related risks.

MBTech's HR team soon recognized potential compliance risks arising from inconsistent HR policies and procedures across their international offices. The risks included unequal employee treatment, breach of labor laws, potential fines, and reputational damage. It became imperative for MBTech to view HRM in a strategic light - to ensure compliance, manage risks, and support business growth.

MBTech began by developing standard HR policies and procedures across all operations, focusing on commonly sensitive areas such as recruitment practices, compensation, benefits, termination protocols, and workplace safety. Electronic HR systems were implemented to automate functions such as time tracking, payroll, benefits administration, and performance management. The system was designed to flag any inconsistencies in real time, making risk identification proactive rather than reactive.

To navigate the complexities of global labor law compliance, MBTech partnered with legal firms in each of their operational countries, ensuring localized expertise and guidance. Furthermore, they invested in compliance training and education for all their employees to embed a culture of compliance throughout the organization.

MBTech has since experienced significant improvements. Their standardized HR policies and procedures ensured fair, consistent, and lawful employee treatment worldwide – strengthening employer-employee relationships.

A real-time risk detection system allowed proactive risk management, reducing the financial and operational consequences of unpredictable HR crises.

This case study reinforces that compliance and risk management need to be strategic priorities in contemporary human resource management. A proactive, globally aware, and systematized approach is vital to managing risks, ensuring compliance, and ultimately, upholding organizational reputation and success in the 21st century.

For organizations such as MBTech looking to future-proof their HR strategy, here are a few recommendations:

1. *Develop robust, standard HR policies and procedures grounded in global best practices but flexible enough to be localized.*

2. *Leverage HR technology for automated compliance-related processes and real-time risk detection.*

3. *Foster a company-wide culture of compliance. This includes routine compliance awareness and training sessions for all employees.*

4. *Seek expert guidance to navigate complex labor laws, especially if operating on a global scale.*

This strategic approach to HR management could prove fundamental in an era where complexity and change are the only constants. It not only safeguards organizations from potential pitfalls but can also serve as a major driver of organizational growth and success.

Compliance & Risk Management in Contemporary SHRM: A Biblical Perspective

As we venture further into the 21st century, this role is becoming even more critical as organizations grapple with a host of complex challenges ranging from environmental sustainability to digital transformation, regulatory compliance, and organizational restructuring, among many others.

Biblically, this perspective stems from the principle illustrated in Luke 14:28-30, KJV, where Jesus taught about counting the cost before constructing a tower to ensure that resources and strategies are in place to complete it. Likewise, strategic human resources management in the 21st century calls for careful planning and consideration of all potential risks and compliance requirements before initiating or adopting specific strategies.

One of the prime aspects of risk management in strategic human resources is compliance management. It embodies aligning the company's practices with legal prescriptions offered by different authorities. In the words of Romans 13:1 (KJV), " Let every soul be subject unto the higher powers. For there is no power but of God: the powers that be are ordained of God." This essentially means observing and adhering to all legal stipulations – local, national, and international – that regulate business operations, labor relations, and workplace environment takes precedence above any other strategic consideration.

For example, fair labor standards, equal employment opportunity, workplace safety and health norms, among others, need to be incorporated into the HR policies and procedures. Any failure not only results in legal sanctions but also leads to reputational damage and loss of trust among employees and other stakeholders, underscoring how compliance and risk are intertwined.

Biblical wisdom offers compelling insights into enhancing risk management strategies in contemporary HR practices. The book of Proverbs, known for its wisdom literature, serves as a practical guide in this respect. Proverbs 22:3 (KJV) notes that, " A prudent man foreseeth the evil, and hideth himself: but the simple pass on, and are punished" Applying these principles, HR management can proactively address potential risks by fostering a culture of awareness, preparedness, and diligence.

Value creation should not be pursued at the expense of value-adherence. The human resources team must help an organization stay true to the moral and ethical values that underpin its vision, mission, and strategic initiatives. These values should resonate with the Golden Rule (Matthew 7:12, KJV). This universal principle, when applied to HR practices, ensures that organizations treat their most asset – human capital – with respect, fairness, and dignity.

Through a biblical lens, risk management and compliance boil down to the core values of responsibility, stewardship, integrity, respect, and ethical leadership. Living out these values forms an integral part of strategic HR management as it leads to a resilient organization, a healthy work environment, and sustainable business success. Proactively identifying and mitigating potential risks, fostering a culture of compliance, and embedding biblical principles into daily business operations can contribute to strengthening the HR risk management framework, ultimately creating a wholesome, value-driven organization that shines its light in the 21st-century business world.

Chapter 16: Reasonable Accommodations in Contemporary SHRM

As businesses continue to evolve, adapt, and build inclusivity, contemporary SHRM must incorporate the provision of reasonable accommodations to employees. This not only manifests a commitment to employee well-being but also stands as a legal obligation under the Americans with Disabilities Act (ADA) and other similar legislation globally.

In essence, 'reasonable accommodations' is a term that refers to alterations or adjustments employers make to the work environment or processes that effectively assist an employee with a disability to perform their job functions. Such modifications are in place to ensure equal employment opportunities for individuals regardless of their physical or mental capabilities.

Why is this Relevant to SHRM?

The basis of SHRM is the development of human capital to drive organizational growth and success. Working towards an environment that embraces diversity and inclusivity by offering reasonable accommodations taps into a talent pool that may otherwise go unnoticed. This should not be perceived as an obligation, but rather a strategic asset – a clear reflection of the organization's commitment to robust and equal employment. Moreover, research has shown that organizations providing reasonable accommodation often see a surge in employee morale and productivity. Such positive workplace dynamics significantly contribute towards the achievement of strategic goals.

How to Implement Reasonably

The implementation of reasonable accommodation should be personalized, considering the unique needs of each affected employee. This may extend to physical alterations in the workspace, flexible working hours, modifications in equipment, revised job duties, or even adjustments in company policies.

However, the keyword here is 'reasonable'. It is crucial to maintain balance, ensuring these accommodations do not impose an 'undue hardship' on the organization's operations or financial health. A well-documented process should be in place to handle accommodation requests – from the initial request to review, up to implementation and subsequent monitoring. Open communication plays a significant role in this procedure, ideally involving the employee, HR, medical professionals, and immediate supervisors.

What Does the Future Hold?

With the increasing focus on diversity and inclusivity, reasonable accommodations will continue to hold importance in SHRM. Technological advancements also play a crucial role in this endeavor, showcasing the significant strides in assistive technology that can benefit disabled employees.

In the granular fabric of SHRM, mapping reasonable accommodations alongside business strategy calls for innovation, empathy, and foresight. It is an ongoing journey and a dynamic process, constantly in need of reevaluation and adjustment in sync with the employee's needs and the business's strategic goals.

Investing in a culture that values diversity and inclusivity, reinforced by implementing reasonable accommodations, signifies an organization's commitment to utilizing the potential of its human capital optimally. Beyond legal requirements and operational benefits, it also fosters an organizational environment synonymous with equality, respect, and opportunity for all. It is evident that the theme of reasonable accommodations is much more than a legal obligation; it serves as a cornerstone for contemporary SHRM, shaping inclusive work environments in this ever-evolving corporate landscape.

Reasonable Accommodations in Contemporary SHRM: A Case Study

In the evolving landscape of the 21st-century workplace, strategic human resources management has taken a leading role in fostering inclusivity and diversity. One critical area involves providing reasonable accommodations to employees with disabilities, enabling equal opportunities to participate and succeed in the workplace.

John Millington, a highly skilled computer programmer at TechPioneers Inc., a leader in the technology industry, provides a compelling narrative on reasonable accommodations. Despite being hearing impaired, John's talent is fundamental to the efficient operation of the business. However, his disability posed communication challenges within his team and stakeholders.

Recognizing John's expertise and the importance of fostering an inclusive environment, the HR department started evaluating the scenario to ensure they deliver appropriate accommodations, fostering both John's comfort and performance. They rightly concluded that

John didn't require preferential treatment but the 'right' working environment to excel.

In collaboration with high-level management, HR decided to invest in advanced ASL (American Sign Language) interpretation software to facilitate communication during meetings. Additionally, they provided John with a special Telecommunication Device for the Deaf (TDD), enabling him to effectively communicate over phone calls. Furthermore, HR came up with the idea of 'Sign Language Lessons' bi-monthly for those interested. The response was overwhelming! Not only did employees develop a new skill, but it also meant John didn't have to depend solely on technology to communicate with his colleagues.

Finally, they implemented ongoing disability sensitivity training programs to educate employees about diverse disabilities and how to interact respectfully with colleagues who have them. These workshops were not a one-off affair but strategically infused into the corporate calendar, reinforcing that inclusivity wasn't a separate initiative but an integral part of the organization's culture.

Implementing reasonable accommodations didn't just make John's life easier but also enriched the work environment, promoting inclusivity and diversity. In realizing the importance of strategically integrating reasonable accommodations into HR practice, the company saw a rise in overall employee morale, productivity, and decreased turnover rates. It also enhanced the company's brand image, garnering commendable views from clients, shareholders, and the industry for its inclusive ethos.

Stories like John's are becoming more common as businesses acknowledge the power of diversity and its positive impact on innovation, creativity, and performance. By aligning reasonable accommodations into strategic HR practices, companies not only fulfill their legal obligations under the ADA (Americans with Disabilities Act) but also drive business progression through inclusivity.

In essence, reasonable accommodations are not just about closing the gap between able-bodied employees and those with disabilities but about leveling the playing field and fostering a culture where everyone feels valued and respected for their unique abilities and contributions. In an era where the war for talent is fierce, businesses adopting strategic accommodations stand to gain considerable competitive advantage – in talent acquisition, retention, and achievement of corporate goals.

Reasonable Accommodations: A Biblical Perspective

In the milieu of contemporary strategic human resources management, reasonable accommodations constitute an essential part of ethical administration. These accommodations not only encompass physical adaptations to workplace environments for individuals with disabilities but also concern the sensitivities and values of a diverse workforce. It is crucial to view this strategy against the backdrop of an emerging global culture that prizes inclusivity and respect for individual dignity above all.

From a Biblical perspective, reasonable accommodations align with the God-given mandate to "...Thou shalt love thy neighbour as thyself..." (Mark 12:31, KJV). Moreover, they reflect the seminal tenet of Christian ethics of preferential care for the weak, as Jesus reminded in His Sermon on the Mount, "Blessed are the merciful: for they shall obtain mercy" (Matthew 5:7, KJV).

Employers who implement a policy of reasonable accommodation send a potent signal that they value each employee as an individual, regardless of their capabilities or circumstances. By creating an environment that is sensitive to employees' unique needs and respectful of their rights, employers can promote the physical, emotional, and spiritual wellness of their workforce. This approach is a practical form of love in action, a direct extension of the Biblical command to "Let love be without dissimulation.

Abhor that which is evil; cleave to that which is good." (Romans 12:9, KJV).

However, while accommodations may be merited and beneficial, it is essential to ensure they are reasonable and do not put undue strain on the employer or other employees. This is in line with the Apostle Paul's exhortation to the Thessalonians: "And that ye study to be quiet, and to do your own business, and to work with your own hands, as we commanded you; that ye may walk honestly toward them that are without, and that ye may have lack of nothing." (1 Thessalonians 4:11-12, KJV).

Hence, the concept of reasonable accommodation is a Biblical construct and Christian business leaders must strive to replicate this model in their workplaces. By doing this, they create an environment that not only adheres to

Christian principles but also aligns with the tenets of contemporary HRM. Consequently, in the context of 21st-century SHRM, reasonable accommodation carried out responsibly and judiciously, can be a compelling tool for fostering a culture of inclusivity, respect, and mutual care. This resonates with the Biblical worldview and the teachings of Christ, an exemplar of love, mercy, and justice.

Chapter 17: Balancing Religious Accommodations in Contemporary SHRM

In the dynamic landscape of the 21st century, businesses are finding themselves at the intersection of diverse cultural, religious, and social perspectives. As an essential facet of global diversity, religious accommodation in the workplace has emerged as a crucial aspect of this evolving mosaic. Going hand in hand with equal employment opportunity laws and set against the backdrop of SHRM, this issue has woven itself deeply within the fabric of workplace discourse.

Effective SHRM strategies have never been more pressed to delicately balance the scales between a company's operational needs and the individual religious rights of its employees. Indeed, the proactive accommodation of employee religious observances is not only a demonstration of ethical leadership but also a strategic investment. It's a statement that advocates for an inclusive work culture, promotes employee engagement, and attracts a wide talent pool by providing a safe, respectful environment for all, regardless of varying faith backgrounds.

Contemporary HR practitioners need to adopt a proactive stance, thus avoiding the risk of costly litigation or employee disengagement. This can manifest in several ways, such as acknowledging religious holidays, granting flexible work schedules for religious observances, or allowing clothing items related to religious affiliations. These accommodations, although seemingly nominal, resonate powerfully with employees, fostering an environment where they can feel seen, valued, and respected.

Balancing Religious Accommodations in Contemporary SHRM: A Case Study

Consider the case study of a high-profile technology company that aptly navigated the tricky terrain of religious accommodation. A Muslim employee requested a slight modification to their work schedule to accommodate a daily prayer ritual. In response, HR crafted a flexible work plan allowing the individual to balance their religious obligations without impacting their ability to meet the responsibilities of their role. The action, although small, reverberated throughout the organization, leading to improved engagement, retention, and job satisfaction scores within the team and larger department.

Conversely, consider the litigation cost incurred by a manufacturing company that refused a similar request for modification in work hours from an employee observing the Sabbath. The employee, feeling discriminated against and unwanted, brought a lawsuit against the company. The cost wasn't only financial, but the company also suffered damage to its reputation, impacting on its attractiveness to a diverse range of potential candidates.

From strategic and legal standpoints, it is incumbent upon HRM to embrace the discourse on religious accommodation actively. This entails understanding the diverse religious practices within the workforce, leveraging legal counsel to stay updated on ever-evolving laws revolving around religious rights and accommodation, and building a robust policy that supports employees' religious needs while maintaining operational integrity.

As globalization continues to converge differing beliefs and practices within the corporate arena, managing religious accommodation effectively remains one of the key challenges 21st-century HRM faces. However, as it continues to evolve, organizations that use strategic HRM to create a more inclusive, respectful workplace will undoubtedly be better poised to attract and retain diverse talent.

Overall, religious accommodation within the workplace is an essential component of every business's diversity and inclusion strategy. It takes an investment of time and resources, but when navigated strategically, can offer vast rewards in employee satisfaction, improved company culture, and better business outcomes. These benefits undeniably affirm the importance of integrating religious accommodation within strategic human resource management.

A Biblical Perspective on Religious Accommodations in Contemporary SHRM

In the ever-evolving contrivance of contemporary workplaces, the principle of religious accommodation is no longer an option, but a necessity. Organizations in the 21st century are witnessing unprecedented diversity amongst employees, where multiple belief systems coexist. Founded from a biblical perspective, the strategic accommodation of these religious diversities is a pivotal undertaking for human resources management (HRM).

In the Bible, the Apostle Paul underlines in (1 Corinthians 12:12-27, KJV) the concept of the body with many parts, each being critical to the functioning of the whole. This teaches us the significance of everyone's contribution, irrespective of their differences - a principle that holds true in the current business milieu.

Further to that, the bible teaches that the responsibility of employers goes beyond tolerating religious diversity to actively facilitating it. This is echoed in Matthew 7:12, also known as the Golden Rule, which instructs to "do unto others what you would have them do unto you." Translated into HRM practice, this means creating a work environment that embraces all religious beliefs, fostering spaces for prayers, acknowledging religious holidays, and integrating practices that cater to religious dietary restrictions, amongst others.

In addition, religions often shape an individual's value system, and these values in turn influence their work ethic - a facet HRM cannot overlook. The Apostle Paul, in Ephesians 6:5-9, emphasizes the importance of employee-employer relationships. HRM should understand that religious accommodations not only serve as an organizational advantage that promotes an inclusive work environment but also boosts employees' morale and work ethics.

Religious accommodation starts at the recruitment and selection stage. Carefully drafted job descriptions and requirements can ensure an absence of religious discrimination. The Bible, in Acts 10:34, sensibly asserts, that God does not show favoritism, and this notion should be extended to the recruitment and selection process.

Bearing in mind the biblical perspective on religious accommodation, it's incumbent for HRM to actively promote religious accommodation strategies. The Bible's teachings are perennial and espouse an ideology of respect and acceptance of diversity. These biblical principles, when implemented strategically, will lead to an HRM that is more productive, and more inclusive, in line with the 21st-century ethos of diversity and inclusion. Remember, employees are the cornerstone of any organization, and their religious beliefs are an integral part of their identity that should be respected and accommodated.

Chapter 18: HRIS and Advanced Technology Integration in Contemporary SHRM

Human Resource Information Systems (HRIS) and Advanced Technology Integration have transformed the landscape of human resource management in the contemporary corporate world. The strategic implementation of these modern tools has brought efficiency, accuracy, and agility in HR operations which are critical for the success of 21st-century organizations.

Making information accessible and organized has always remained a core objective of a company's HR department. Thanks to HRIS, this has now become more efficient and less time-consuming. HRIS offers a centralized repository of employee data which simplifies the process of record-keeping, data retrieval, and decision-making. This system eliminates the need for manual record-keeping and ensures accurate and readily available data, thereby significantly reducing paperwork and administration load.

Moreover, HRIS streamlines daily HR operations like recruitment, training, performance management, benefits administration, timesheet tracking, and more. It automates these processes, minimizing errors, improving consistency, and enabling HR professionals to focus more on strategic tasks such as recruitment planning, strategic initiatives, policy development, and employee engagement.

In addition to HRIS, the integration of advanced technologies like Artificial Intelligence (AI), Machine Learning (ML), business analytics, and Big Data has revolutionized HRM. AI, for instance, is being used to automate resume screening, schedule interviews, predict employee attrition, and much more. On the other hand, ML algorithms can analyze vast amounts of data and predict hiring trends, training needs, employee performance, and so forth.

In recent years, the use of business analytics in HRM has also seen a significant rise. With this technology, HR departments can predict workforce trends, analyze recruitment channels, evaluate the impact of HR policies, and optimize HR practices in alignment with company objectives. Big Data technology, with its ability to process and analyze massive amounts of unstructured data, has allowed HR professionals to make informed decisions, derive meaningful insights, and devise effective HR strategies.

The effective integration of advanced technologies with HR practices requires an undeniable strategic approach. Companies must ensure appropriate investment, choose suitable technology platforms or providers, and prepare their HR staff to adapt to these changes. Training and development programs should be employed to enhance employees' technological skills and capacities. Moreover, organizations should also focus on dealing with potential challenges such as data privacy and security issues, ethical considerations, and the risk of bias in AI-based decision-making models.

Interestingly, HRIS and advanced technology integration have emerged as significant game-changers in the strategic human resources management landscape of the 21st century. Organizations willing to stay competitive in this dynamic business environment must embrace these innovations and efficiently adapt to these technological shifts as an integral part of their SHRM.

HRIS and Advanced Technology Integration in Contemporary SHRM: Case Study 1 & 2

Case Study 1: Human Resource Information System (HRIS) Application

Company A is a fast-growing national retail organization with over 5,000 employees. The traditional, semi-automated HR processes led to inefficiencies, inaccuracies in data management, and significant delays in retrieving employee information. Realizing the limitations of their existing system, company A opted for HRIS implementation.

The implementation of the HRIS transformed their HR functions remarkably. The system introduced a wide range of HR functionalities including recruitment, onboarding, payroll, performance management, and training modules, improving efficiency, productivity, and decision-making.

The data accuracy significantly improved, as manual data entry was eliminated. Data could be accessed in real-time which supported faster decision-making processes. HRIS also allowed for better grievance handling through a seamless and effective employee self-service portal. This directly contributed to increased employee satisfaction and reduced attrition rates.

By automating manual tasks, HRIS empowered the HR team to focus more on strategic tasks. The implementation of HRIS led to a reduction in human errors and labor cost-driven savings. It also helped the HR department in forecasting and strategically planning manpower requirements, by providing analytics and trends.

Case Study 2: Advanced Technology Integration in HR Management

Company B, a multinational manufacturing firm with a diverse workforce of over 20,000 employees, faced issues in HR procedures owing to its size and diversity. The prime issues included complexities in talent acquisition and management, employee engagement, payroll, and benefits administration.

The answer lies in the integration of advanced technologies like Machine Learning (ML), Natural Language Processing (NLP), and Predictive Analytics within their HR functions. The resulting system wonderfully combined the potency of ML and NLP to improve candidate sourcing, talent management, and employee engagement.

ML algorithms significantly improved the recruitment process by effectively grading candidates based on certain parameters, resulting in the recruitment of suitable candidates. Predictive analytics offered insights into employee performance trends, aiding in planning training and development programs.

Employee self-service portals using NLP made interactions and grievance redressal more effective and efficient. The payroll and benefits administration also significantly improved by using cloud-based applications and predictive analysis for benefits optimization.

Integrating advanced technologies provided highly effective HR solutions to company B. A measurable improvement was noted in HR operations, decision-making process, and overall employee experience, ultimately resulting in a highly satisfied and productive workforce.

These two real-world case studies demonstrate how embracing advanced technologies can optimize human resources management in the contemporary corporate world. By innovatively integrating HRIS and AI technologies, businesses can effectively manage their workforce, increase operational efficiency, reduce costs, improve decision-making, and enhance employee satisfaction.

HRIS and Advanced Technology Integration in Contemporary SHRM: A Biblical Perspective

The evolving domain of HRM, particularly in the 21st century, has taken a paradigm shift from traditional methods to more strategic, electronic-based systems known as HRIS–

leveraging advanced technology for efficiency, productivity, and effectiveness. This discourse seeks to link this modern evolution in HRM to age-old wisdom from the biblical perspective.

Understanding HRIS and Advanced Technology Integration

HRIS is an integrated system designed to help provide information used in HR decision making such as payroll, time and labor tracking, benefits administration, and performance record, among others. This crossbreeding of HR and IT sectors has necessitated the proper alignment of HR policies and practices with the overall strategic organizational goals using technology. However, this technological incorporation must not overlook the human element to ensure a work environment that cherishes human dignity, respect, and fairness - virtues deeply entrenched in biblical teachings.

Biblical Perspectives on HRIS

In Colossians 3:23 (KJV), the Bible guides workers to, "And whatsoever ye do, do it heartily, as to the Lord, and not unto men;" From this standpoint, HRIS as a management tool comes as an enabler, not a replacement. It equips HR professionals to execute duties with increased precision, efficiency, and effectiveness, thereby cultivating a work culture of excellence as outlined biblically.

Advanced Technology Integration: A Biblical View

Technology in HRM should be seen as an opportunity to showcase good stewardship – a principle we find in the Parable of the Talents

(Matthew 25: 14-30, KJV). This parable conveys the importance of using one's resources wisely. From an HRM perspective, technology is a valuable resource that must be utilized effectively to reap maximum benefits.

Moreover, technology integration in HRM can reflect the biblical emphasis on justice, fairness, and respect for human dignity. Systems that ensure equitable pay structures, fair recruitment and selection processes, and unbiased feedback mechanisms are such examples. They are reminiscent of the biblical teaching in Proverbs 16:11, which underscores fair transactions and treatment.

Applying Biblical Teaching to Contemporary HRM Practices

Implementing HRIS and advanced technological solutions aids in strategic decisions, resource allocation, and performance management and helps foster a culture of fairness, dignity, and mutual respect. However, these systems must be steered by HR professionals who are conscious of providing sustainable work environments that foster human dignity, spirit, and personality as suggested in Genesis 1:27.

HRIS and advanced technology integration bear the potential to revolutionize work systems. Nonetheless, while strategizing these systems, it is crucial to understand the value of human dignity, justice, fairness, and stewardship as prescribed in biblical teachings. In this alignment lies the perfect symbiosis of age-old wisdom and contemporary practices. Thus, the tech-enhanced evolution of HRM, coupled with the vision of human-centric biblical perspectives, leads to a holistic model of HRM - one that is timely and timeless.

Part II: Contemporary SHRM Application in the Public Sector

SHRM has rapidly evolved over the past decade and has gradually emerged as a highly recognized disciplinary field that plays a significant role in organizational performance. One of the sectors that benefit greatly from the applications of SHRM is the public sector. Unlike the common perception, public organizations too, deal with the complexities of managing human resources in today's diverse, dynamic, and digitalized world.

The contemporary application of SHRM in the public sector involves a more strategic and future-oriented approach. Public sector organizations are now increasingly implementing strategies aimed at having the right people, with the right skills, in the right roles, at the right time.

This approach helps to eliminate skills gaps, proactively address future workforce needs, and align staff resources to meet the service delivery requirements.

In addition to recruitment, SHRM applications in the public sector also include initiatives for talent retention, knowledge management, diversity and inclusion, and employee well-being. For instance, many public organizations are developing onboarding and mentoring programs to inspire new hires, build a sense of belonging, and promote employee retention. They are also creating platforms for knowledge sharing and continuous learning to encourage knowledge transfer and career development. Furthermore, with increasing traction for inclusive workplaces, public sector organizations are adopting more holistic approaches to diversity and inclusion. Lastly, public sector organizations are focusing more on preventing job burnout and promoting employee's physical and psychological health through various well-being initiatives.

Another noteworthy trend is the increasing use of data analytics in public HRM. Public sector organizations are becoming more sophisticated in the utilization of HR metrics, predictive analytics, and big data to make evidence-based decisions about human resources. Such a data-driven approach allows for better workforce planning, talent management, performance management, and policy formation.

Moreover, in today's digital era, public sector organizations are also leveraging technology to modernize HR processes. The use of digital tools and platforms allows for more efficient recruitment, performance evaluation, training and development, and employee engagement. Also, amidst the pandemic-induced shift to remote working, public sector organizations have been quick to adapt to virtual HRM strategies.

However, implementing SHRM in the public sector is not without challenges. Public organizations typically operate with public scrutiny, bureaucratic procedural norms, strict legislation, budgetary constraints, and political influences, which often limit the flexibility and innovativeness of their HR practices. Therefore, public organizations need to carefully design and execute their SHRM strategies to meet the unique needs and constraints of the public sector.

Overall, the contemporary SHRM practices in the public sector have indeed transitioned from a traditional administrative role to a more strategic role. Public sector HR leaders are now playing fundamental roles in strategic planning and enhancing organizational effectiveness. While there are certainly complexities and challenges, the benefits of SHRM unarguably outweigh the concerns and present a compelling case for its wider adoption in the public sector.

Chapter 19: Contemporary SHRM in the U.S. Federal Government

The public sector, like its private counterparts, has an immense need for effective and efficient human resource departments, but the specific requirements make SHRM in the federal government context a unique case.

Human resources in the federal government sector are a substantial asset, but they remain underutilized due to outmoded and inefficient management strategies. The evolving workplace environment calls for a contemporary and strategic approach to HRM, one where organizational objective meets employee satisfaction for the mutual benefit of all parties.

SHRM plays a critical role in this equation. It is a holistic, strategic approach that integrates employee sentiment, career growth, and development with broader organizational goals. It emphasizes the value of human capital by aligning HRM strategies with the overall objectives and direction of the organization.

The federal government, known for its bureaucratic and hierarchical model, is notorious for its slow responses to change, including developments in HRM. However, incorporating SHRM could institute a profound shift in this mindset and propel the government sector forward to improve operational efficiency and productivity.

From a talent management perspective, the federal government faces significant challenges due to its rigid structures and policy-bound operations which lead to lower employee morale and productivity. By incorporating contemporary

SHRM applications, it can develop flexible approaches that not only attract competent personnel but also retain and professionally develop them.

Moreover, SHRM can function as a tool for succession planning within the federal government, as it recognizes and nurtures potential leaders for future roles. A clear understanding of this potential highlights the need to invest in employee development. Furthermore, SHRM, with its emphasis on worker satisfaction and career development, can help the federal government create a more positive public image. By employing rigorous employee selection and retention practices, maintaining a diverse and inclusive environment, and offering competitive remuneration and benefits, the government can demonstrate its commitment to its workers' welfare, thereby enhancing its reputation.

Overall, the strategic application of SHRM in the public sector is not mere speculation – it offers tangible benefits to the federal government. By incorporating modern HRM strategies, the government can foster a more engaged, competent, and satisfied workforce, ultimately contributing to its overall efficiency and effectiveness.

Contemporary SHRM Application in the U.S. Federal Government: Case Study

SHRM plays a pivotal role in the federal government sector to streamline practices, improve service delivery, and maintain a motivated staff. It is the nexus that combines human resource management (HRM) with strategic goals to improve business function. This case study delves into the contemporary application of SHRM in federal government agencies, particularly the U.S. Department of Labor (DOL).

Strategies and Challenges

One of the critical shreds of evidence of SHRM at play is the Job Corps program, a free career training program strategized by the DOL for young people. A critical component of SHRM is equipping people with the requisite skills for organizational growth. This Job Corps program fits this mandate perfectly as it improves workforce quality by providing relevant skills for job market demands.

However, the federal government faces a unique challenge in achieving SHRM objectives -

employee diversity. With a workforce as diverse as the U.S. government's, meeting every individual's needs becomes challenging. To address this, the government implemented Equal Employment Opportunity (EEO), a policy that promotes workplace diversification that adheres to the SHRM's principle of equality and fairness.

Transformations and Innovations

Recently, the government has been prioritizing technology integration in HRM, which plays into the broader SHRM framework. For instance, the use of HR analytics supports strategic planning and decision-making. Parallelly, digitalization has streamlined recruitment and hiring processes, contributing towards a more efficient strategic HR function.

Concurrently, there remains space for improvement. For example, while the government is continuously working towards technology adoption, the pace is relatively slow compared to the private sector. Overcoming challenges associated with bureaucratic limitations can catalyze digital transformation in the federal HRM sphere.

Impact and Results

Despite these challenges, certain noteworthy achievements uphold the robustness of SHRM in federal departments. The Department of Veterans Affairs, for instance, significantly improved its human capital strategy with the Veterans Employment Initiative, leading to better job placements and higher satisfaction levels among veterans.

Conclusion

SHRM in the federal government is a testament to the strategic alignment of HR policies with organizational goals. Despite facing unique challenges, federal agencies are making headway into innovative methods promoting strategic HRM practices. These endeavors, alongside lessons learned, offer valuable insights to other governmental and non-governmental entities seeking to shore up their HR strategies. Excellent human resource strategies equate to enhanced service delivery, which remains the goal of any government agency.

Contemporary SHRM Application in the U.S. Federal Government: Biblical Perspective

SHRM in the context of the federal government requires an understanding of how to create an environment that empowers employees, fosters good ethical behavior, and promotes efficient management practices. This can be viewed through a biblical perspective where principles such as fairness, integrity, human dignity, and responsibility are highly valued.

1. **Fairness**: The Bible teaches us the importance of fair treatment in numerous verses including Colossians 4:1 (KJV), "Masters, give unto your servants that which is just and equal; knowing that ye also have a Master in heaven." This adherence to fair treatment can be applied to SHRM in the federal government where each employee, regardless of their position or role, should be given equal opportunities for advancement and should be assessed based on performance without bias.

2. **Integrity**: On individual and organizational levels, integrity is another principle that can drive SHRM processes. Proverbs 10:9 (KJV) highlights, " He that walketh uprightly walketh surely: but he that perverteth his ways shall be known." This implies the necessity of honest, transparent, and open communication throughout the management process. Providing clear expectations, and feedback, acknowledging the accomplishments, and addressing any issues or conflicts directly can foster an atmosphere of trust and respect in the working environment.

3. **Human Dignity**: SHRM should also encompass the principle of upholding human dignity. Genesis 1:27 suggests that everyone possesses tremendous innate value and thus should be treated with respect and dignity. High regard for employee well-being, personal

development, work-life balance, and safe working conditions are ways SHRM can uphold this principle.

4. **Responsibility**: From a biblical standpoint, we are taught to take responsibility for our actions. In the corporate landscape, and particularly in SHRM, responsibility is crucial. Managers should be held responsible for their decisions and the outcomes of these decisions. This is not only applicable to decision-making but also to managing people.

 The Bible gives us an illustrative framework that contains principles that are highly applicable to SHRM in a federal government context. By treating employees fairly, operating with integrity, preserving human dignity, and taking responsibility for actions, a positive, efficient, and ethical working environment can be fostered.

These principles are not only beneficial for personal moral development, but they hold the ability to enhance overall organizational success in the long term.

Chapter 20: Application of SHRM in State Government

In today's dynamic operational environment, the application of Strategic Human Resource Management (SHRM) has become a crucial aspect of every organization, including those in the public sector like state governments. This memorandum provides an overview of how SHRM could be implemented in the domain of state government.

The primary objective of SHRM is to align the human resource (HR) strategy with the overall goals and objectives of the organization. In the case of state governments, the goals primarily revolve around serving the public interest, enforcing laws, and enhancing the social welfare of the community.

The contemporary challenges faced by state governments, including employee turnover, budget constraints, an aging workforce, and significant changes in technology, demand a more strategic approach to managing human resources. Modern SHRM concepts like talent management, change management, and workforce planning can be potent tools for addressing these challenges.

To begin with, talent management can help state governments in attracting, retaining, and developing potential workforce. Amidst a competitive labor market, a strategic approach is necessary to attract top talent. This could require the formulation of competitive benefits and compensation packages and providing growth opportunities with a secure working environment - key differentiators in public sector employment.

Linked to talent management is the concept of change management. The increasing speed of changing government protocols and technologies necessitates equipping employees with the skills needed to adapt quickly. Regular training programs, workshops, and seminars can help employees improve their skills and stay abreast with the latest trends and changes. Integrating change management into SHRM can help reduce the resistance to change and enhance employee adaptability.

Workforce planning, another crucial aspect of SHRM, involves a strategic approach to predicting future labor needs and preparing for them. It is particularly relevant for state governments grappling with an aging workforce. Effective workforce planning can help in identifying future vacancy trends, developing plans for staff retirement, and building succession plans.

Lastly, the principles of inclusivity and diversity must be woven into the fabric of SHRM to ensure fair treatment of all employees. Reflecting society, state governments should consciously ensure that their workforce is representative of the communities they serve.

To conclude, the application of SHRM in the context of state government has the potential to radically transform the way human resources are managed. It is a forward-looking, proactive approach that aligns the people strategy with the state government's aim of serving its community better.

Remember, a well-managed human resource is synonymous with a well-administered state government. A shift toward strategic human resource management can significantly contribute to state governments' efforts toward operational excellence and enhanced public service delivery. As an HR consultant, I recommend state government entities initiate a detailed review of their current HR practices and consider the adoption of SHRM for optimized manpower planning and management.

SHRM Application at the State Government Level: Case Study

SHRM is a pivotal approach in an entity's administrative functioning, that aligns human resources (HR) management with the overall strategic objectives of the organization. Despite being extensively implemented in corporate entities, its application in the public sector, more specifically at the state government level, requires adept study due to the distinctive dynamics of such public establishments. This case study will investigate the contemporary SHRM application at the State Government of California, recognized for its advanced HR practices.

Background

The California state government constitutes several departments, each with unique HR practices. However, the lack of a unified SHRM strategy led to inconsistencies, reduced employee motivation, and a lack of direction. These contribute to a lag in adopted best practices, thereby striking the need to implement SHRM.

SHRM Implementation

The introduction of a contemporary SHRM plan by the State Personnel Board aimed to consolidate diverse HR practices across all departments and align them with the state's strategic objectives. The primary aspects of the SHRM included workforce planning, talent acquisition and management, performance management, and employee engagement and learning development.

Each department was required to align its HR practices with the strategic objectives by creating department-specific SHRM strategies. Following this, a multi-tier review structure was implemented for cross-validation across various departments, ensuring adherence to the centralized SHRM strategy.

Outcomes and Analysis

After SHRM implementation, the state government observed a substantial improvement in employee engagement, productivity, and a consistent rise in overall performance metrics. Furthermore, the improved workforce management led to the successful accomplishment of the state's strategic objectives.

However, a few challenges were encountered in terms of resistance to change, initial implementation cost, and the time needed for the full assimilation of SHRM practices. Nonetheless, these challenges were overcome with a planned change management strategy, fiscal allocation, and adequate time provisions, highlighting the effective management of HR at the state level.

Conclusion

The California State Government's case exhibits the transformative influence of SHRM application in the public sector. Despite the substantial heterogeneity among various departments, a uniform SHRM policy has capacitated the tackling of numerous HR challenges, boosted productivity, and enabled a strategy-driven, efficient administrative mechanism.

The case study thus demonstrates that SHRM's implementation at the state government level significantly contributes, when coupled with strategic vision and proactive management. The strategic implementation of HR demands a unique approach, emphasizing the need to identify department-specific challenges and opportunities. Therefore, the applicability of SHRM in the public sector role is magnified and holds substantial potential for the future. This case study lays the foundation for public establishments to utilize SHRM for achieving strategic objectives and enhancing public administration performance.

Biblical Perspective and Its Relevance to Contemporary SHRM Applications in State Government

It is undeniable that the concepts and principles rooted in the Bible can offer a profound influence on ethical comportment and moral compass, providing valuable insights for the implementation of strategic human resource management (SHRM) at the state government level. While there may exist differences in religious beliefs, the bible's central principles of justice, love, equality, and respect underscore a universally acceptable ethical framework.

The gospel's teachings translate into fostering a workforce culture that esteems all workers irrespective of their backgrounds (Galatians 3:28) - a remarkably contemporary stance in line with the tenets of equal employment opportunities and diversity inclusivity, heavily underlined in modern SHRM.

Just as outlined in Proverbs 16:3 (KJV), " Commit thy works unto the Lord, and thy thoughts shall be established," translates to acknowledging the importance of strategic planning in the public sector. It indicates that organizations, including state government agencies, should prioritize setting clear, strategic goals while asking for divine direction at all stages. Devising a strategic plan invested in employee development, training, engagement, and the establishment of fair reward systems not only improves overall organizational performance but also aligns closely with biblical teachings (Luke 14:28-30).

Another key biblical principle is 'loving your neighbor as yourself' (Mark 12:31), which significantly resonates with employee relations in SHRM. It signifies promoting respect, empathy, and understanding between employees, thereby cultivating a conducive working environment. In the increasingly diverse makeup of the public sector, this principle becomes the backbone of fair treatment, anti-harassment, and non-discrimination policies.

In the book of Colossians 3:23 highlights the need to work diligently, not for men's praise but for the fulfillment that comes from performing tasks robustly. This verse fortifies performance-driven cultures, advocating for employees who work tirelessly to accomplish their goals, congruent with modern performance management systems.

Following wise leadership in the Bible, leaders should serve with humility and not lord authority over subordinates (Matthew 20:26-27). This servant leadership style emulates an ethos of mutual respect and collaboration, fostering a team-oriented workforce that aligns with effective change management and leadership philosophies in modern SHRM.

Lastly, the Bible stresses honesty (Proverbs 12:22), which aligns with transparency and accountability in human resource management paradigms. These virtues should be depicted in procurement processes, implementing fair hiring and promotion procedures, and maintaining open communication channels within the workforce.

It is discernible that the Bible is not only religious rhetoric but a reservoir of moral and ethical standards applicable in public sector SHRM. Integrating these principles can promote a dutiful workforce, foster a healthy workplace climate, and even boost public trust in state governments while enhancing overall state performance.

Chapter 21: Contemporary SHRM Application at the Local and Municipal Government Levels

SHRM is an essential aspect of administration that aids organizations, including those in the public sector such as local and municipal levels of government, in achieving their short and long-term goals. In the public sector, SHRM helps in overcoming challenges associated with retaining skilled employees, maintaining service levels, dealing with budget constraints, and managing change effectively.

SHRM in this context encompasses the systematic alignment of people with strategic goals and objectives to enhance organizational performance. It ensures the availability and capacity of the workforce, skill development, employee motivation, and fostering an innovative work environment. More contemporary applications focus on the integration of HR strategy with overall organizational strategy, being more inclusive, employee-centric, and data-driven. At the local and municipal government levels, the following applications of SHRM are observed:

1. **Strategic Workforce Planning**: Local governments are increasingly using strategic workforce planning to ensure they have the right people in the right place at the right time. This includes a strong focus on succession planning and talent management to deal with retirements and to ensure capacity for the future.

2. **Employee Engagement and Wellness Programs**: To reduce turnover and improve job satisfaction, many local governments are implementing employee engagement and wellness programs as part of their HR strategy. This

includes policies focused on work-life balance and mental and physical health.

3. **Performance Management**: Increasing demands for accountability and transparency in the public sector have led to increased focus on performance management within HR strategy. This includes setting clear expectations, providing regular feedback, and recognizing good performance.

4. **Training and Development**: As part of their SHRM, many local governments are focusing on employee training and professional development to improve skills, capacity, and productivity. They also promote continuous learning and improvement, and the use of technology for skill enhancement.

5. **Diversity and Inclusion**: Acknowledging the changing demographic landscape, local governments are striving to create a more diverse and inclusive workplace. A part of SHRM, this aims at respecting and appreciating differences in ethnicity, gender, age, nationality, disability, and sexual orientation among others.

Implementing strategic HRM at the local and municipal levels is crucial in ensuring public sector organizations remain competitive, achieve their goals, maintain a motivated workforce, and provide excellent service to citizens. The evolution of SHRM in the public sector now focuses on creating a work environment that not only embodies the present-day needs of the employees but even goes a step further, making the organization future-ready. Therefore, dynamic modifications in the SHRM process to suit contemporary needs are increasingly becoming the norm rather than the exception.

SHRM at the Local and Municipal Government Levels: Case Study

This case study highlights the critical role of SHRM in local and municipal government sectors with real-life examples.

Scenario: Local Municipality X

Our subject is Municipality X, which was plagued with inefficiencies and low motivation levels among staff members. These issues were affecting service delivery and local citizen satisfaction levels. Municipality X decided to embrace a more strategic approach to their HR management to address these issues and increase overall productivity.

Strategic HRM Application:

Municipality X started by aligning human resources plans with their overall strategic objectives. They understood the importance of people as their most vital resource, so they focused on hiring, training, and empowering HR personnel who could drive these changes. They also initiated a comprehensive skills analysis to understand staff capabilities better and identify any gaps in skills.

Results:

1. **Improved Performance**: Municipality X noted improved institutional performance levels after the implementation of SHRM. Key Performance Indicators (KPI) results showed a significant uptick, and the staff demonstrated higher levels of productivity.

2. **Increased Staff Retention**: Municipality X experienced less attrition, due to policies focusing on employee well-being and satisfaction. A more streamlined recruitment process meant that the best-qualified candidates were being hired and retained.

3. **Enhanced Public Satisfaction**: One of the pivotal measures of success for any government entity is public satisfaction. After SHRM implementation, Municipality X observed a substantial increase in citizen satisfaction due to improved service delivery.

Scenario: Local Government Y

The next case study involves Local Government Y, which was struggling with succession planning and staff development to ensure future leadership continuity.

Strategic HRM Application:

Local Government Y adopted a strategic approach to build a leadership pipeline, focusing on talent identification, development, and succession planning. They integrated these plans with strategic objectives to ensure future leaders would be aligned with the organization's goals and cultural values.

Results:

1. **Leadership Development**: A developed leadership pipeline and pathways for career progression led to an increase in employee morale and job satisfaction.

2. **Successful Transitions**: With a robust succession planning system, leadership transitions occurred smoothly, ensuring minimal disruption to the organization's strategies and initiatives.

3. **Long-term Sustainability**: Focusing on talent development and succession planning enabled Local Government Y to ensure long-term sustainability and progress, with capable leaders ready to drive the organization forward.

Conclusion:

In both adopted scenarios, strategic human resource management proved invaluable. Implementing and applying SHRM practices at local and municipal government levels yielded improved performance, higher staff retention, increased public satisfaction, and ensured leadership continuity and organizational sustainability. Therefore, it is recommended that similar organizations adapt their HR practices from administrative to strategic, aligning them with the overall organizational goals. This transition to a strategic approach in human resource management will help ensure their competitiveness and effectiveness in serving their constituents.

SHRM Application at Local and Municipal Government Levels: A Biblical Perspective

The application of SHRM at modern-day local and municipal government levels must be guided by principles deeply rooted in the Bible. The biblical perspective implies adherence to the unchanging values of Christianity like fairness, compassion, integrity, and human dignity. This document explores the intersection between the tenets of the Bible and modern SHRM practices.

Biblical Principle 1: Fairness and Equality – The Parity Principle:

The Bible emphasizes equal treatment and fairness. In SHRM, this principle expresses itself in practices such as unbiased recruitment, fair job evaluations, and equitable compensation. The Book of Proverbs 11:1 promotes equal opportunity to all potential and existing staff in local and municipal governments, regardless of their background, gender, race, or disability status.

Biblical Principle 2: Integrity – The Honesty Principle:

Integrity as seen in the biblical context is honesty, transparency, and high moral standards. It is motivated by the scriptural injunction in Proverbs 10:9 (KJV) "He that walketh uprightly walketh surely: but he that perverteth his ways shall be known." In human resource management, these moral compasses are depicted through transparent performance evaluations, maintaining confidentiality, and adherence to set ethical standards. Integrity in SHRM emphasizes the importance of truthfulness in dealing with every human resource aspect.

Biblical Principle 3: Compassion and Considerate – The Empathy Principle:

Colossians 3:12 sets out a clear mandate for those who lead, "Put on therefore, as the elect of God, holy and beloved, bowels of mercies, kindness, humbleness of mind, meekness, longsuffering." HR practitioners must display compassion when dealing with staff challenges, offering support, mediating conflicts, and providing accommodation when necessary. Such actions establish a supportive working environment that helps employees thrive and remain motivated.

Biblical Principle 4: Human Dignity – The Respect Principle:

Grounded on Genesis 1:27 the respect principle calls for honoring the sacredness of all humans. From a SHRM perspective, this underscores the necessity to treat employees with respect, honor, and dignity. It highlights the importance of building healthy relationships, avoiding favoritism, and treating each person as a valued entity.

Conclusion:

The Bible offers valuable insights that can be integrated into contemporary SHRM practices. By aligning SHRM with the principles of fairness, integrity, compassion, and human dignity, local and municipal governments can improve their HR practices, promote a more ethically conscious workforce, and drive their jurisdictions toward achieving their mission, vision, and goals. Therefore, it is prudent that local and municipal governments draw from these principles, creating a workplace culture that is inclusive, supportive, and harmonious.

Chapter 22: Contemporary SHRM: A PESTEL Framework

Strategic Human Resources Management (SHRM) does not exist in isolation but is influenced by external factors: Political, Economic, Social, Technological, Environmental, and Legal (PESTEL). Today's dynamic and rapidly evolving business environment makes it more imperative to understand these influences and their effects on SHRM.

Political factors influence SHRM through legislative and regulatory changes. Government policies often drive organizational practices. For instance, changes in labor laws, public sector reforms, and affirmative action can impact recruitment, selection, training, and benefits. Organizations should anticipate political changes and proactively design their HR strategies to ensure compliance and competitive advantage.

Economic factors play a critical role in SHRM. Economic downturns or upturns can affect the availability of human capital, the ability of an organization to attract and retain talent, and the overall cost of labor. In an uncertain economy, SHRM can help organizations remain resilient by investing in employee development, flexible work arrangements, and comprehensive benefits packages that accommodate employees' changing needs.

Social factors, including cultural norms, demographic trends, and societal values, have a profound effect on SHRM. For example, an aging workforce and increasing cultural diversity necessitate a more inclusive approach to HRM. Moreover, societal expectations concerning work-life balance, health and wellness, and corporate social responsibility have led to innovative HR practices.

Technological advancements bring about changes in the type of skills required and the nature of work, leading to alterations in staffing, training, and development strategies. The rise of remote work, for instance, demands new managerial skills and employee engagement methods. SHRM must leverage technologies like AI and analytics to enhance talent management, performance measurement, and strategic decision-making.

Environmental considerations are becoming crucial in SHRM. Organizations are compelled to incorporate sustainability into their strategy, which influences HR practices like green HRM. Environment-friendly practices attract talent who value social responsibility, impacting talent acquisition and retention.

Lastly, legal factors like employment laws, health and safety regulations, and standards on equality amongst the workforce, guide the policies structured by HR departments. It hence requires HR to stay current with local, regional, and international legislation and understand their implications on the organization.

To conclude, the PESTEL framework provides a larger context, and understanding its influence on SHRM brings a comprehensive outlook on external challenges and opportunities. Keeping HR strategies aligned with PESTEL factors ensures an organization's readiness for future uncertainties and helps it sustain a competitive edge. Managing human resources is not merely an internal administrative function; instead, it requires a strategic vision that encompasses a wide range of external influences. It is critical for modern HR practitioners to understand the complex and interconnected world in which they operate and to factor these considerations into their HR strategies.

Leveraging SHRM through the Lens of PESTEL Analysis: A Case Study of UR Badging Systems Pvt. Ltd.

UR Badging Systems Pvt. Ltd., a well-regarded Security Solutions firm based out of Ohio, USA, has been grappling to manage its Human Resources effectively. The company, in its quest to outpace competitors, had overlooked the importance of strategic human resource management (SHRM), leading to increased employee turnover, falling productivity, and waning customer satisfaction.

Political Factors:

Regulations and political stability play an integral role in shaping the company's SHRM approach. Politically, UR Stands to benefit from the Ohio state government's newly introduced regulations favoring tech and cyber-security firms. However, the regulations also entail stringent staff hiring guidelines and implications on immigration policies due to federal laws. For UR, this means adopting an innovative SHRM approach to hire appropriately skilled domestic workers and providing them with the requisite job security.

Economic Factors:

The US economy's relative stability, supported by the external funding environment for tech startups, provides UR with an opportunity to revamp its SHRM policies. With financial resources at their disposal, they can offer better compensations, subsequently attracting and retaining talent through incentive-based remunerations and benefits. It will provide an economic advantage and boost workforce morale and productivity.

Social Factors:

Cultural implications, demographic changes, and societal trends influenced UR's SHRM. As a culturally diverse company, the strategy was adapted to support diversity and inclusivity. The increasing number of millennials and Gen Z in the workforce made flexible working hours, remote working, and employee wellness programs a significant part of the SHRM plan.

Technological Factors:

Rapid changes in technology affect the skill sets required for jobs, thus impacting SHRM. UR, being a technology firm, had to incorporate perpetual learning and development into its SHRM. This involves constant upskilling and cross-skilling of employees to prevent skill obsolescence and ensure the firm's ability to keep up with industry trends and innovations.

Environmental Factors:

Increasing awareness about sustainability and environmental conservation had an impact on the SHRM policies of UR. The company implemented green HRM strategies such as reducing paper use, switching to renewable energy, and encouraging sustainable practices. This not only made UR appealing to socially responsible candidates but also contributed towards a better brand image.

Legal Factors:

Compliance with employment laws and other legal factors is crucial for any successful SHRM. UR had to ensure its policies aligned with the Fair Labor Standards Act (FLSA), Occupational Safety and Health Administration (OSHA) guidelines, and other local labor and employment legislation, ensuring its HR policies were legally compliant.

Conclusion:

The case of UR Badging Systems illustrates the importance of PESTEL factors in shaping SHRM. A well-calibrated blend of political, economic, social, technological, environmental, and legal factors has led to a more comprehensive, inclusive, and compelling strategy. The results, though initial, are promising, with signs of increased employee engagement, reduced turnover, and improved productivity. Businesses increasingly need to adopt a holistic approach to SHRM – as UR has shown, an approach that responds to PESTEL cues can offer a formidable competitive edge.

SHRM within a Contemporary Context: A Biblical Perspective Examined through the PESTEL Framework

As an HR Advisor, tasked with demonstrating a biblical perspective on SHRM, one must consider the admonition given in 1 Peter 5:2-3 (KJV), " Feed the flock of God which is among you, taking the oversight thereof, not by constraint, but willingly; not for filthy lucre, but of a ready mind; neither as being lords over God's heritage, but being examples to the flock." This principle underscores the importance of stewardship for all HR professionals. The PESTEL framework builds on this foundational concept, shedding light on how political, economic, social, technological, environmental, and legal factors shape SHRM.

POLITICAL: Titus 3:1 (KJV) reminds us to "Put them in mind to be subject to principalities and powers, to obey magistrates, to be ready to every good work" Herein lays the principle of ethical conduct. SHRM professionals must be aware that political decisions can have lasting implications on businesses. This includes a broad range of issues from globalization to specific governmental policies. Maintaining ethical behavior amidst these ever-changing circumstances is essential in both building trust and ensuring employees' welfare is prioritized.

ECONOMIC: The biblical worldview encompasses the responsible use of resources. Proverbs 27:23-24 (KJV) advises, "Be thou diligent to know the state of thy flocks and look well to thy herds. For riches are not for ever: and doth the crown endures to every generation?" This counsel speaks to the need for HR management to cultivate a keen understanding of the economic factors affecting the organization and workforce. Economic volatility calls for prudent decisions that not only preserve resources but also uphold the dignity and welfare of employees.

SOCIAL: The Bible strongly encourages fair treatment and respect for every individual illustrated in Galatians 3:28. The 21st-century workplace is increasingly diverse, and the HR leadership's role is to foster inclusivity and equality, irrespective of employees' social, cultural, or demographic backgrounds.

TECHNOLOGICAL: As we navigate the fourth industrial revolution, Proverbs 19:2 (KJV) suggests, "Also, that the soul be without knowledge, it is not good; and he that hasteth with his feet sinneth." It's essential to balance the enthusiasm for technology adoption with a full appreciation of its implications. From privacy issues to remote working transitions, HR's role in discerning and facilitating the responsible use of technology has never been more critical.

ENVIRONMENTAL: We are stewards of creation, as evidenced by Genesis 2:15 (KJV), " And the Lord God took the man, and put him into the garden of Eden to dress it and to keep it." As organizations strive for sustainability, SHRM practitioners must promote working conditions and business strategies that align with safeguarding God's creation.

LEGAL: Romans 13:1-2 (KJV) teaches us to "Let every soul be subject unto the higher powers. For there is no power but of God: the powers that be are ordained of God. Whosoever therefore resisteth the power, resisteth the ordinance of God: and they that resist shall receive to themselves damnation." HR teams must ensure the organization's compliance with labor laws and other regulations. The aim is not merely to avoid legal repercussions; it's part of our accountability to higher principles to uphold justice, integrity, and fairness in the workplace.

Finally, these contemporary SHRM perspectives are a reminder of the broader calling of HR professionals, echoed in Matthew 7:12. Providing a workplace that is economically sound, socially fair, technologically equipped, environmentally conscious, and legally compliant in line with the golden thread of biblical ethics—is in fact what we all yearn for.

The PESTEL analysis offers a comprehensive framework that allows HR professionals to respond wisely to a rapidly evolving environment. However, the value and power of these strategic adjustments stand or fall on the commitment to biblical ethics that truly serve the best interest of the entire workforce.

Chapter 23: SHRM Outlook & Trends in 2024 and Beyond

Strategic Human Resources Management (SHRM) has become a critical pillar of growth, progress, and longevity for organizations worldwide. As we move forth into 2024 and beyond, a drastic shift from traditional HR management to a more strategic role can be envisaged.

The future of SHRM will be characterized by technological advancements, data-driven decision-making, and employee-centric practices. Technologies like Artificial Intelligence (AI) and Machine Learning (ML) will play a pivotal role in automating administrative tasks, thereby freeing HR professionals to focus more on strategic roles. Furthermore, these technologies will help in proactive decision-making by predicting workforce trends and behaviors based on prior patterns.

Data will be at the heart of future SHRM practices. Companies will invest massively in Big Data analytics to gain valuable insights about their employees and use this information strategically. These insights would aid in understanding the factors affecting employee morale, retention, and productivity, enabling HR managers to align their strategies effectively.

The nature of work is also transitioning - it's becoming more flexible, remote, and diverse. In such a scenario, HR strategies would be designed to accommodate these changes, and we can anticipate a considerable rise in workforce diversity and inclusion initiatives. These strategies will be crucial in maintaining workplace harmony and increased productivity.

Since businesses nowadays operate in an extremely dynamic environment, SHRM needs to equip itself with risk management capabilities. HR managers of the future need to foresee potential threats and risks and incorporate suitable risk management strategies. This is especially vital in unforeseen circumstances like the recent COVID-19 pandemic.

Another game-changer would be the future of Learning & Development (L&D) in SHRM. In the face of constant technological advancements, organizations need to ensure that they are well-equipped with a digitally adept workforce that can adapt to these changes seamlessly.

Employee well-being will also become a strategic priority. More than a mere duty of care, employee well-being will be viewed as a strategic concern tied to long-term organizational success.

SHRM applications will therefore extend beyond traditional working hours and days, recognizing that employee well-being affects individual productivity, team cohesion, and overall business success.

Finally, the entrenched notion of a 'global mindset' will continue to gain importance. SHRM will focus on promoting this global perspective to leverage talent from diverse backgrounds and cultures to foster innovation and adapt to the changing business landscape globally.

The future of Strategic Human Resources Management will be more dynamic, advancing beyond the traditional HR roles to a more strategic one. As we move into 2024 and beyond, companies should invest heavily in data and technology, promote a more flexible and diverse workforce, focus on employee well-being and learning and development, and foster a global mindset. These trends represent both challenges and opportunities for HR professionals, and their ability to navigate through these changes will significantly impact organizational success in the future.

Chapter 24: Epilogue

Throughout this book, the author explores the intricacies of Strategic Human Resource Management (SHRM), highlighting its comprehensive nature, adaptability, and vital role in the modern business environment. We conclude this journey by exploring a theological perspective; a lens that allows us to examine SHRM against the backdrop of biblical teachings.

The Bible may seem disconnected from the contemporary business world, but upon further reflection, one discovers key principles that align fundamentally with today's SHRM practices. These core concepts can offer rich wisdom and guidance, steering organizations towards ethical, fair, and conscientious decision-making grounded in a religious context.

At the core of the Bible's teachings are the concepts of love, respect, and fairness. Underneath these principles is the Bible's affirmation of human dignity, which takes front stage in SHRM's people-centric approach. Strategic human resource management is not merely about aligning an organization's human resources with its goals, but also about considering the holistic wellbeing of employees.

In today's business environment, the challenge lies in merging biblical principles with business strategies. The Bible instructs us to 'love your neighbor as yourself' (Mark 12:31) and to 'do unto others as you would have them do to you' (Matthew 7:12). These declarations align with the thrust of SHRM, advocating fair treatment and fostering healthy, constructive relationships in the workplace.

These biblical principles speak directly to the organizational climate, which is a core component of SHRM. An organization's ethical values, culture, and leadership play a significant role in shaping its work environment. The Bible encourages leaders to 'shepherd the flock of God that is among you, exercising oversight, not under compulsion, but willingly, as God would have you' (1 Peter 5:2). This encourages servant leadership – a model premised on putting others' needs first, which is aligned with the principles of SHRM.

Furthermore, the Bible addresses the contentious subject of conflict management, which is a key focus in SHRM. In the book of Romans, the Apostle Paul urges followers to "live peaceably with all" (Romans 12:18), advocating for a workplace that is harmonious and free from unnecessary strife. This biblical principle reaffirms the role of SHRM as a mediator in conflict resolution, ensuring all parties are treated with dignity while maintaining organizational harmony and productivity.

Although there is an inherent complexity in integrating religious tenets into corporate strategies, adopting a biblical perspective on SHRM fosters a deep-seated respect for humanity and promotes ethical practices in managerial decision-making processes. By aligning strategic human resource practices with biblical principles, leaders can achieve their organizational goals while fostering a spirit of fellowship, righteousness, fairness, and mutual respect within their workforce.

As we close this chapter, it is essential to recognize the potential implications of the Bible's teachings on contemporary SHRM. Through its mosaic of wisdom, the Bible offers invaluable insight into managing human resources - a reminder that amid incessant corporate goals and strategies, people are the organization's most valuable asset.

This biblical perspective on SHRM does not oppose current practices but, instead, reminds us of the importance of grounding these practices in a framework that values human dignity above all. As we strive towards effective SHRM strategies, keeping these principles in mind will create a flourishing workplace environment where people are appreciated and motivated to attain their full potential. This, in turn, ensures sustained organizational growth and success.

Organizations must view employees not just as resources, but as unique individuals cherished and valued by God. SHRM, through a biblical lens, then becomes a powerful tool to shape organizations weaved with threads of compassion, justice, respect, and mutual love - a reflection of God's heart and character.

HR consultants and practitioners, equipped with the knowledge of both SHRM and biblical teachings, have a precious opportunity to sculpt organizations that thrive in their mission while honoring the inherent worth of every individual at their core. Principally, integrating a biblical perspective in SHRM adds a layer of depth that reiterates the fundamental principle underscoring all human resource management: the undeniable value and significance of people.

Glossary of Terms

Accountability: The responsibility an individual or department must execute specific tasks or roles efficiently, competently, and promptly. It signifies an obligation to report on outcomes, whether positive or negative, and to accept consequences in the event of any failures or shortcomings. An accountable party is answerable to stakeholders, and they are expected to act transparently, showing integrity and reliability. It is a key factor that fosters trust and contributes to the smooth running of an organization. This critical attribute promotes performance accountability, individual accountability, and team accountability, all contributing to a healthy workplace culture and improved business performance.

Action Plans: Strategic guides designed to achieve specific goals within a set timeframe.

These plans outline the necessary steps to reach objectives, including essential resources, potential obstacles, and key performance indicators. Action plans are vital because they provide clarity, enable measurement of progress, and foster accountability. Whether setting out plans for individual development, project management, or business improvement, an action plan serves as the blueprint to facilitate goal attainment.

Advocacy: Fostering support for a cause or policy within the organization or externally. This can involve actions like communicating with stakeholders, promoting initiatives, engaging in proactive organization-related conversations, influencing decisions, or guiding policy changes with an objective to align and promote the company's interests.

Affirmative Action: A set of policies and practices within a government or organization, seeking to increase the representation of particular groups based on their historical and social identities such as race, religion, gender, and sexual orientation. The aim is to foster diversity and equal opportunity, while seeking remediation for historical social injustices. This policy is enforced in multiple domains such as education, employment, and business.

Agility: An organization's ability to rapidly adapt to market and environmental changes in productive and cost-effective ways. It encompasses responding quickly to changing customer needs, competitors, and industry trends while maintaining or improving business operations. Agile companies excel in identifying and seizing opportunities more swiftly than competitors, thus ensuring longevity and relevance in an unpredictable business landscape.

Algorithms: A set of instructions designed to perform a specific task. This can be a simple process, such as adding two numbers together, or a complex operation, such as processing data from a large database. Algorithms are the foundation of computer software and are essential for delivering effective business solutions. Efficiency and accuracy are the driving forces behind the use of algorithms in the business world.

Alliance Building: The strategic process where two or more organizations, or teams within an organization, join forces to achieve mutually beneficial business goals. This form of partnership is designed to leverage the unique strengths, resources, and capabilities of the involved entities with an aim to maximize productivity, innovation, and competitive advantage. In the context of human resources, it may involve cross-functional teams, collaborative projects, or strategic mergers between businesses. Alliance Building is integral for fostering corporate cohesion, strengthening operational efficiency, and fueling growth and expansion.

Americans with Disabilities Act (ADA): A comprehensive civil rights law passed in 1990 that prohibits discrimination against individuals with disabilities in all areas of public life, including employment, transportation, public accommodation, communications, and governmental activities. It is designed to provide equal opportunities, equitable access, and prohibits discriminatory practices to ensure a level playing field for all. The ADA applies to employers with 15 or more employees and requires reasonable accommodation for employees with disabilities.

Artificial Intelligence (AI): The simulation of human intelligence processes by machines, especially computer systems. These processes encompass learning, reasoning, problem-solving, perception, and language understanding. In essence, AI is the development of computer systems adept at executing tasks typically requiring human intellect.

Attrition: A natural reduction in the workforce due to normal factors like retirement and resignation.

Baby Boomers: Individuals born post World War II, during the period of increased birth rates globally, typically between the years 1946 and 1964. These individuals are known for being hardworking, resourceful, and have a strong work ethic. They have witnessed a variety of economic climates and technological advancements, which gives them a unique perspective in the workforce.

Benchmarking: A process of comparing one's business processes and performance metrics with the industry's best.

Bias: A predisposition or a preconceived opinion that favors one side or perspective over another, ultimately influencing fair judgment. It can be unconscious or conscious and is often associated with prejudice, stereotyping, and discrimination. Bias, particularly in the workplace, can lead to skewed decisions in hiring, promotion, and employee development, thereby undermining the principles of diversity, equity, and inclusion. It's crucial to identify and address these biases to ensure fair treatment and equal opportunities for all employees.

Biblical Lens: The perspective through which individuals interpret their experiences, the world around them, and their decision-making processes, grounded in the teachings and principles found in the Bible. It means allowing one's perception, understanding, and actions to be guided by Biblical values. This profound approach promotes ethical behavior, integrity, compassion, and justice, among others, that align with professional standards. It can positively influence the workplace culture, interpersonal interactions, and decision-making processes.

Biblical Worldview: A philosophical perspective that interprets the entire world, including societal structures, human behavior, and natural phenomena, through the lens of the principles and values found in the Bible. It profoundly influences an individual's understanding of fundamental aspects like purpose, identity, and morality. This worldview thrives on the belief that all events, both historical and contemporary, have theological significance as per the Christian faith.

Big Data: A term that describes extremely large data sets that may be analyzed computationally to reveal patterns, trends, and associations, especially relating to human behavior and interactions. It can include structured and unstructured data, gathered from various sources and often in real time. Big Data is a vital asset for businesses today as it provides deep insights that drive strategic decision-making.

Brand Reputation: The way a brand is perceived by its customers, stakeholders, and the market. It is built over time through a combination of factors including product quality, customer service, corporate ethics, public relations, and marketing efforts. A strong brand reputation can add significant value to a business, supporting customer loyalty, and providing resilience in competitive markets.

Budget Constraints: The financial limitations that a firm must consider during its decision-making process. They set financial boundaries that limit a company's ability to spend on hiring, retaining, and maintaining employees. These constraints typically include categories such as salary rates, benefits packages, training costs, and office expenses. Thus, it is essential for companies to prioritize spending in alignment with their strategic goals, while being cognizant of these financial limits to manage responsibly and effectively.

Bureaucratic: A system of administration characterized by rigid adherence to rules, a hierarchy of authority, and formalized procedures. In a business context, a bureaucratic structure relies on specific job roles, a high level of management control, and a clear chain of command down through the organization. While it can provide stability and clarity, it can also produce inefficiencies due to lack of flexibility and innovation.

Burnout: A state of prolonged physical, emotional, and mental exhaustion often associated with chronic workplace stress. Characterized by feelings of energy depletion or exhaustion, increased mental distance from one's job, feelings of negativism or cynicism towards the job and reduced professional efficacy, it can lead to decreased productivity, low morale, and high employee turnover. Effective prevention and intervention strategies should be in place to foster employee well-being and engagement.

Business Analytics: The use of statistical methods, data analysis, and quantitative methods to analyze and interpret data. It involves extracting meaningful insights from raw data to aid decision-making. Areas covered include predictive analytics, prescriptive analytics, and reporting. These insights help optimize business practices, enhance efficiency, and improve strategic decision-making, driving businesses toward achieving their objectives.

Collaborative Learning: A strategic approach in which team members actively engage in a common task. This approach creates an environment where each participant's contribution is valued and hones their collective problem-solving skills.

Compensation Protocols: The systematic guidelines that a company follows to determine the financial benefits and salaries of its employees. The protocols usually involve factors such as job analyses and evaluations, performance management and appraisals, and regulatory compliance. Implementing a robust compensation policy helps to attract, retain, and motivate high caliber professionals and encourages employees to perform at their best.

Contemporary: Forward-thinking, innovative, and aligned with the current state of the industry or market. This term is frequently used to compare or contrast old and new methods or theories in business.

Competency Mapping: Identifying the specific skills, knowledge, abilities, and behaviors needed to operate effectively in a specific trade, profession, or job position.

Competitive Environments: The dynamics that exist when companies within the same industry vie for the same resources and customers. It is characterized by numerous factors such as intensity of competition, number of competitors, pace of market evolution, and customer's bargaining power. Understanding this environment is crucial for strategic planning and decision-making as it affects a company's competitive advantage and profitability.

Competitive Remuneration: A comprehensive compensation package offered to an employee, which is at par with or better than the standard industry rates. It encompasses various elements like base salary, bonuses, benefits, and incentives. The intention is to attract, retain, and motivate high-quality employees in a competitive job market.

Compliance Management: The process through which organizations ensure adherence to a set of predetermined guidelines, laws, regulations, and business operations. It involves identifying relevant regulations, establishing controls to support compliance, testing these controls, and taking corrective actions whenever necessary.

Change Management: A systematic approach and application of knowledge, tools, and resources to deal with change and achieve the desired business outcome. It involves managing the transition in people, processes, and technology from a current state to a desired future state to realize the organization's strategic objectives as efficiently and effectively as possible.

Code of Conduct: A set of principles that guide an organization's decisions and overall operations. It defines what an organization considers right and ethical behavior, providing guidelines for professional conduct. The Code outlines specific behaviors that are required or prohibited and is designed to protect the organization, its employees, stakeholders, and the general public. It helps uphold the organization's reputation while also ensuring transparency and fairness in its processes. It underpins the expectations for employees' behavior in the workplace, and in their dealings with customers, suppliers, partners and competitors.

Conflict Resolution Training: Structured programs designed to equip employees with the necessary skills and knowledge required to manage and resolve conflicts effectively. This training plays a crucial role in fostering an environment of mutual respect and understanding within a workplace, leading to enhanced productivity and positive employee dynamics.

Communication Channels: The mediums through which information is exchanged within an organization. They are classified into two major types: formal and informal communication channels. Both types of channels play vital roles in the effectiveness of an organization's communication strategy, and it is crucial for businesses to effectively manage these channels to ensure smooth and efficient communication.

Competency-Based Job Design: An approach where job descriptions are structured around the competencies, skills, knowledge, and abilities vital for the successful performance of a job. This design focuses on the outcomes or results of a job rather than simply the tasks or activities involved. Its purpose is to align the job demands with the employee's skills and competencies to enhance job satisfaction, and engagement, and hence, boost productivity. The process involves identifying and defining the core competencies and their subsequent incorporation into the various components of HR functions such as recruitment, performance management, training, etc.

Competitive Environments: The dynamic external system in which businesses compete for resources. It includes factors such as the number and relative strength of competitors, customers, suppliers, and the threat of new entrants or substitutes.

Computer-Based Learning: E-learning or online learning, is a type of education where students use computers or digital devices to access educational material and learn new concepts. It incorporates a variety of learning resources, such as videos, interactive lessons, digital assessments, online discussions, and more. One of its main advantages is the flexibility it offers, as learners can often complete the material at their own pace and according to their own schedules. It's also known for its scalability, being able to effectively instruct a large number of students simultaneously, irrespective of geographical disparities.

Demographic Trends: Shifts in population characteristics within a certain geographical area over a specific period of time. These characteristics may encompass age, gender, marital status, income level, educational attainment, employment status, among others. Understanding these trends is crucial to organizations as they impact labor supply, consumer demand, and business strategies. This knowledge aids in developing effective HR policies, workforce planning and enhancing organizational growth.

Digitalization: A strategic and operational shift that involves the utilization of digital technologies to transform a business's model and provide new revenue and value-producing opportunities. This process integrates digital information into various areas of an organization, fundamentally changing how it operates and delivers value to its customers.

Digital Platforms: Software applications that use technology to enhance processes, increase efficiency, and improve productivity. These online solutions can be implemented across a range of business areas, covering everything from communications and collaboration to project management, task automation, data analysis, and reporting. Utilizing such tools often results in streamlined operations, improved workflows, reduced human error, and significant cost savings.

Digital Transformation: The integration of digital technology into all areas of a business, fundamentally changing how you operate and deliver value to customers. It's a shift that requires organizations to continually challenge the status quo, experiment, and get comfortable with failure. It impacts not just technology but also the culture, people, and processes.

Diversity and Inclusion (D&I): An integral part of human resources strategy, fostering cultural competence, encouraging diverse thought, and enhancing organizational performance.

Diversity Management: A strategy to promote the perception, acknowledgment, and implementation of diversity in a workplace environment.

Downward Communication: Are the policies, directives, and instructions that are sent from higher levels within the organization to lower levels.

Efficiency: The ability of an organization to deliver products or services in the most cost-effective manner possible without sacrificing quality. It is an optimal use of resources – time, money, and manpower – to achieve the desired output. High efficiency translates to lower costs, increased profitability, and maximized customer value. Enhanced operational efficiency is often synonymous with enhanced business competitiveness.

Egalitarian Group: A group that ensures equality for all its members, irrespective of race, gender, wealth, or social status. It promotes equal rights, equal opportunities, and equal treatment. There is a shared belief in the inherent value of each individual and this principle is upheld by fair laws and policies that do not favor any specific group over another. It is structured on the premise that all individuals are worthy of the same respect, dignity, and opportunities for growth. This creates a balanced, inclusive environment conducive to social harmony and personal development.

Empathy: A critical leadership skill that involves the ability to understand and share the feelings of another individual. It refers to the ability to perceive others' thoughts and emotions, allowing for improved communication and team cohesion in a workplace setting. It should not be confused with sympathy, which refers to feeling sorry for others. Instead, empathy involves comprehending others' experiences and responding to them appropriately—an essential factor in fostering a positive and harmonious work environment.

Employee Engagement: A workplace approach that results in the right conditions for all members of an organization to give their best each day.

Employment Legislation: Laws set out by the government regarding the terms and conditions of employment.

Employee Morale: The overall outlook, attitude, satisfaction, and confidence that employees feel at work. When employees are positive about their work environment and believe that they can meet their most important career and vocational needs, employee morale is positive or high.

Employee Relations: The management and maintenance of relationships between an organization and its employees. This encompasses actions to ensure a positive work environment, effective communication, fair treatment, and resolution of conflicts.

Employee Self-Service Portals (ESS): Digital platforms that empower employees to independently manage a range of HR-related tasks such as updating personal information, applying for leave, viewing salary history, and accessing benefits information. By automating these administrative tasks, ESS portals promote efficiency, accuracy, and streamline HR workflows allowing the HR department to focus on strategic activities.

Employee Turnover: The percentage of workers who leave an organization and are replaced by new employees during a defined period. This key HR metric can be a significant cost for a company, considering the expenses involved in hiring, onboarding, productivity loss, and the potential impact on morale and team performance. High employee turnover often signals issues engrained within the organizational culture or workplace environment. Therefore, understanding, measuring, and addressing this metric is critical for organizational health and sustainable success.

Environmental Sustainability: The responsible interaction with the environment to avoid depletion or degradation of natural resources and allow for long-term environmental quality. It involves making decisions and taking action that are in the interests of protecting the natural world, with particular emphasis on preserving the capability of the environment to support human life.

Equal Employment Office (EEO): A federal agency that enforces laws designed to prevent discrimination in the workplace. These laws cover all aspects of employment, including hiring, firing, promotions, job duties, wages, and benefits. The EEO safeguards individuals from employment discrimination based on race, color, religion, sex, national origin, disability, and age. It upholds fair and just workplace conditions and is committed to fostering diversity within the workforce.

Equality: The even-handed treatment of all employees without any form of discrimination. This means that every staff member should be given equal opportunities for growth, advancement, and decision-making. The concept also includes a fair and unbiased approach regarding compensation, hiring, training, promotions, and terminations. The end goal is to cultivate a workplace environment that respects and values diverse backgrounds and perspectives.

Ethics: The principles that guide actions and behaviors within an organization. These principles include honesty, transparency, fairness, respect for others, obeying the law, social responsibility, and safeguarding individual and corporate integrity. They fundamentally dictate how businesses operate, engaging with stakeholders and making decisions that not only benefit the company but also positively impact society. Ethics in the workplace are vital as they help in maintaining a positive working environment, boosting employees' morale, and enhance trust and cooperation among employees and management. In essence, the presence of strong ethical standards signifies the moral compass that every organization needs to thrive sustainably.

Ethical Comportment: The demonstration of behavior that is aligned with moral principles, integrity, honesty, respect, and professionalism. Those displaying ethical comportment adhere to standards that usually surpass basic legal requirements, ensuring the fair and dignified treatment of all persons in a business setting. It also involves consistent ethical decision-making, responsibility, and accountability for one's actions.

Ethical Leadership: The practice of leading in a manner that respects the rights and dignity of others. It is about integrity, honesty, and transparency in all actions and interactions. Ethical leaders are role models who inspire by means of a persuasive vision, and drive inspiration around shared goals. They foster an environment where employees feel valued and rewarded fairly for their contributions. Key qualities of ethical leadership include the ability to make fair decisions based on justice and equality, they further promote an environment where openness and truthfulness are encouraged. Fundamentally, the ethical leadership approach improves organizational atmospheres, enhances employee engagement, motivation, and contributes significantly to corporate social responsibility efforts.

Ethical Standards: Clearly defined guidelines that organizations and individuals follow to maintain honesty, integrity, and professionalism. They encompass a wide range of conduct, including respect for diversity, transparency in decision-making, commitment to meeting obligations, and avoiding any form of misconduct. Ethical standards serve as a foundation for building company culture and promoting a harmonious working environment.

Ethos: The guiding beliefs or ideals that characterize a community, nation, or ideology. It's the set of concepts that influence an individual's or a group's behavior, attitudes, and understanding of what is deemed appropriate or in line with their overall mission and values. Ethos is effectively realized through consistent behaviors, communication, and attitudes that align with these defined values and beliefs. In a business environment, establishing a strong ethos Is essential to cultivate a positive company culture and build trust both internally and externally. It acts as a framework guiding everyday operations and strategic decisions. Therefore, 'Ethos' is not just a belief system, but it contributes significantly to shaping the identity and reputation of an organization.

Executive Compensation: The remuneration package provided to top-level management officials within an organization. This typically includes a combination of salary, bonuses, shares, options, and various other incentive-based rewards. The primary goal of executive compensation is to align the interests of senior executives with those of the shareholders, motivating the executives to perform at their highest capacity to increase company value. The structure and components of executive compensation are often complex, designed with careful consideration to balance immediate rewards with long-term organizational growth. Furthermore, they can vary widely amongst organizations, influenced by factors such as company size, industry, and overall business strategy.

Fair Labor Standards Act (FLSA): A federal law in the United States that establishes minimum wage, overtime pay, recordkeeping, and youth employment standards affecting employers and employees in the private sector and in federal, state, and local governments. It is an essential legislation that upholds the rights of workers nationwide.

Feedback Mechanisms: Essential tools utilized within an organization to gauge the effectiveness of processes, functions, or employees' performance. These mechanisms provide an efficient means for information to be analyzed, which subsequently guides improvements, adjustments, or reinforcement of success. Feedback can be gathered through various platforms including surveys, face-to-face meetings, performance evaluations, suggestion boxes, and customer feedback. The key to an effective feedback mechanism is providing a safe space where stakeholders feel confident to speak honestly and constructively. These mechanisms should not merely identify weaknesses but also highlight strengths to stimulate the replication of success throughout the organization. Feedback should be considered from all angles and from all stakeholders including employees, management, and external customers to foster a comprehensive understanding of the organization's effectiveness. By continuously assessing and refining feedback mechanisms, organizations can positively influence employee morale, enhance performance efficiency, and improve overall business productivity.

Flexible Work Arrangements (FWAs): Strategies implemented by businesses that allow employees variation in their work structure. These modifications can encompass alterations to the time, location, and way an employee's work gets completed. FWAs often include practices like remote working, flexible timing, compressed workweeks, and job-sharing. By employing FWAs, organizations aim to promote work-life balance, improve job satisfaction, and attract a diverse talent pool, ultimately leading to higher productivity.

Fringe Benefits: Benefits given by employers to employees in addition to their regular salaries, like health insurance, 401K match, etc.

Formal Communication Channels: Established by the organization and are typically documented and well-structured. These can be further segmented into downward, upward, and horizontal communication.

Generation Alpha: Often referred to as the children of millennials, encompasses individuals born from 2010 to 2025. As the first generation entirely born within the 21st century, these individuals are expected to be the most technologically immersed and digitally adept cohort in history, with their lives deeply intertwined with AI, robotics, and other advanced technologies. As such, businesses and educators must strategically adapt to accommodate their learning styles and future workplace expectations.

Generation X: the demographic cohort following the Baby Boomers and preceding the Millennials. Birth years for Generation X typically range from the early-to-mid 1960s to the early 1980s. This group is characterized by its breadth of experience in both traditional and digital workplaces, strong work-life balance pursuits, and a penchant for adaptability in cascading market conditions.

Generation Z: Often referred to as Gen Z, is the demographic cohort succeeding Millennials and preceding Generation Alpha. Represented by individuals born from the mid-to-late 1990s through the early 2010s, they are the latest generation to enter the workforce. In the context of business and human resource management, this generation is recognized for their comfort with technology, having been exposed to the internet, social media, and mobile systems from a young age. Gen Z values creativity, innovation, and XXXxperiences work-life balance differently than previous generations. Understanding these characteristics is vital for effective human capital management, workplace planning, and overall organizational effectiveness.

Globalization: The integration of markets, businesses, and services around the world through advancements in technology, communications, and trade policy.

Global Geopolitics: The study of the effects of Earth's geography – human and physical – on politics and international relations, observed at a global level. It considers the impact of geographical elements like location, size, climate, and natural resources on the strategies and decisions of nations. The understanding of such dynamics is crucial for businesses that operate internationally or wish to expand to different countries. This helps them to make informed decisions based on the political stability, resource availability, and trade policies of different countries.

Governance: The process and structures used to direct and manage an organization's operations and activities. It includes the establishment of policies and procedures, decision-making processes, and accountability frameworks to ensure that an organization is managed effectively and efficiently for the achievement of its objectives. It also encompasses the broader system of control and communication that links those in governance roles, such as the board, senior management, and shareholders, to ensure transparency, fairness, and responsible decision-making.

Grace: A term that refers mainly to an individual's elegance, politeness, style, or manner. In a performance management context, it may be referred to as the consideration period extended to an employee for improving their performance to meet the defined standards. This term also has wide use in theological contexts, denoting unmerited favor or love from a divine entity. However, the interpretation can vary greatly depending on the context.

Green Human Resources Management (GHRM): A strategic approach to business that promotes sustainable use of resources within business operations. It emphasizes the role of

Human Resource Management in promoting sustainability by embedding green behaviors and practices in the workplace. This can include activities such as developing digital skills to eliminate paper waste, promoting teleworking to reduce commuting emissions, and encouraging employees to participate in sustainable initiatives. Green HRM serves both the purpose of environmental responsibility and achieving organizational goals.

Headcount: The total number of employees working in an organization at a specific point in time. It may include both full-time and part-time employees and could also encompass remote workers. Companies use headcount to measure growth, determine budget allocations, and plan future hiring needs.

Health Insurance Portability and Accountability Act (HIPAA): A federal legislation in the United States enacted in 1996. This act promotes maintaining the confidentiality and security of individuals' healthcare data and information, thus preventing any unauthorized access or misuse. In essence, it aims to safeguard individuals' protected health information (PHI) while ensuring the efficient flow of health-related information necessary for quality patient care and other significant public reasons. Any violation of HIPAA regulations would witness severe penalties. Therefore, it's crucial that organizations dealing with PHI fully understand and comply with its standards.

Healthcare Initiatives: Strategies or actions aimed at enhancing the quality, accessibility, and affordability of healthcare services. They may involve implementing new policies, employing advanced technologies, or promoting health awareness programs. These initiatives can be driven by various entities such as government agencies, healthcare providers, or private organizations, with objectives such as improving patient outcomes, promoting preventative care, and addressing public health issues.

Hierarchy: The arrangement of individuals within a corporation according to power, status, and job function. It's essentially a pyramid-shaped structure with the chief executive at the top, followed by other senior executives, middle managers, and rank-and-file employees. This structure helps define the roles and responsibilities of each individual, ensuring efficient operation and management within the organization.

Homogeneous: Teams or groups within the organization that consist of individuals who share similar characteristics like the same race, gender, age, or educational background. This can impact the diversity within an organization, potentially leading to a lack of varying perspectives and ideas.

Horizontal Communication: Occurs between employees of the same or similar levels in an organization.

HR Business Partner (HRBP): A pivotal role in the human resources function. This position serves as a consultant to management on human resources-related issues. The HRBP acts as an employee champion and change agent, with the overall responsibility of aligning business objectives with employees and management at the departmental level. Essentially, the HRBP maintains a high level of business literacy about the business unit's financial position and competition, including plans and its culture. They deeply understand the company's vision and business strategies to provide and execute human capital strategies accordingly.

HR Consultant: A professional who specializes in advising organizations on the efficient management of human resources to optimize productivity, profitability, and overall business performance. They leverage their knowledge of human resource management strategies to analyze the organization's current HR programs and policies, identify opportunities for improvement, and implement effective solutions. Key areas of focus include talent acquisition, organizational structure, employee engagement and retention, training and development, benefits, compensation, and compliance with labor laws and regulations. Their goal is to enhance the organization's ability to attract, retain, and cultivate top talent, while also promoting a positive workplace culture.

HR Manager: An HR Manager is instrumental for any organization as they strategically orchestrate the effective use of personnel to meet organizational goals. Key responsibilities include recruitment and retention, employee development, compensation, and benefits, and ensuring compliance with labor laws. Through their leadership role, they foster positive work culture, resolve conflicts, and manage employee records while aligning human capital with the organization's strategic plan.

HR Metrics: Quantifiable measurements that help HR monitor and assess the efficiency of operational tasks and the overall performance of the workforce. They include factors such as turnover rates, training costs, and average time taken to fill a job vacancy among others. These metrics serve as a valuable tool for strategic planning as they enable the detection of trends, and identification of inefficiencies, and hence, aid in making effective and informed decisions for business progression.

HR Politics: The act of using power and social networking within an organization to achieve changes that benefit the organization or individuals within it. This involves the use of influence to affect decisions within the organization, tactics like strategic networking, information control, alliance building, and creating a favorable image. While HR politics can sometimes have negative connotations associated with manipulative behavior, it can also be viewed positively where it helps in making effective decisions and fostering professional relationships. Thus, managing HR politics is crucial in maintaining a productive and harmonious workplace environment.

Human Capital (HC): The collective skills, knowledge, or other intangible attributes of individuals that can be used to create economic value for the individuals, their employers, or their community. It encompasses factors such as education, experience, abilities, skills, and health. Enhancing human capital involves investing in the education, training, and health of the workforce.

Human Capital Management (HCM): The comprehensive set of practices for recruiting, managing, developing, and optimizing the human resources of an organization. The objective of

HCM is to maximize employee performance in service of an employer's strategic objectives.

Human Dignity: The inherent and intrinsic worth of all individuals, regardless of their status or position within an organization. It underscores the essential principle of respect for individuals and promotes values of fairness, decency, equality, and respect for diversity. Upholding human dignity essentially means treating everyone with respect, integrity, and care, thereby fostering an environment of mutual respect and psychological safety.

Human Resources (HR): To the department within a business that is primarily responsible for all aspects related to the management of employees. This includes recruitment, hiring, orientation and onboarding processes, payroll and compensation strategy, training and development, performance evaluations, benefits and perks management, employee relations, and ensuring compliance with labor laws. Essentially, HR's role is to optimize the use of the human capital (HC) available to an organization to effectively achieve their strategic objectives. HR managers also play a crucial role in shaping company culture and organizational structure.

Human Resources Management (HRM): A pivotal business function that encompasses the strategic planning, managing, and directing of individuals within an organization. This includes overseeing recruitment processes, developing training and development initiatives, ensuring legal compliance, setting company culture, and implementing policies that enhance employee performance and satisfaction. The primary goal of HRM is to enable all employees to contribute effectively and productively to the overall strategic objectives of the organization.

Human Resources Information System (HRIS): An enterprise software solution that integrates and streamlines human resources (HR) management. This technological tool manages employee data, facilitates HR processes, and supports decision-making. Key functionalities typically include recruitment, time and attendance tracking, performance management, benefits administration, payroll, and reporting. The overall objective of an HRIS is to enhance efficiency, productivity, and transparency within an organization's HR function.

Hybrid Work: A flexible work model that combines both remote and in-office work. Rather than having employees work solely from a physical company office or completely remote, this model allows staff to split their time between working from home and working in the office. This approach is adopted to maximize productivity and employee satisfaction by providing flexibility, reducing commute time, and facilitating in-person collaboration as per need.

Incentive-Based Remunerations: A compensation strategy where employees are financially rewarded for meeting specified performance objectives. These rewards, which can include bonuses, commission, and profit sharing, are designed to motivate employees to enhance their work performance and productivity. The structure of this pay scheme varies among organizations depending on their specific business objectives.

Industrial Relations: The management of work-related obligations and entitlements between employers and their employees.

Informal Communication Channels: Also known as the grapevine, are not structured, or regulated. This can include interactions during lunch breaks or casual discussions among employees.

Information Control: The process of managing and controlling the generation, distribution, storage, retrieval, and disposal of information within an organization. This process ensures that all information, such as data, documents, and reports, is accurate and accessible to authorized personnel only. It includes measures to prevent unauthorized access, modifications, or breaches of privacy. Information control, when implemented effectively, enhances operational efficiency, promotes transparency, and safeguards the organization against potential risks associated with information misuse or mishandling.

Innovation: The process of introducing new, unique ideas, services, or products to create value or gain competitive advantage. This strategic approach often involves improving existing procedures or creating solutions to unresolved problems, to boost efficiency and productivity. Innovation is a critical driver for growth and sustainability, encouraging a culture of continuous learning and adaptation in a rapidly evolving business landscape.

Integrated Information Systems: Bring together various types of data and processes from multiple sources into a unified, coherent entity. The primary benefit of these systems is the facilitation of efficient data sharing and communication across different departments or sectors within an organization. By doing so, these systems eliminate the issue of data silos and enable seamless data access for all stakeholders. Furthermore, the integration of various systems can lead to enhanced productivity and decision-making by providing a holistic view of organizational operations.

Integrity: The characteristic of being honest and exhibiting consistent adherence to strong moral and ethical principles and values. In a business context, these principles may encompass reliability, truthfulness, transparency, and robustness of moral judgments. These qualities are essential as they lay the groundwork for trust, thus promoting a positive work environment and strong professional relationships.

Intervention: A coordinated process where specific actions are designed and implemented to enhance effectiveness within an organization. It typically involves identifying problems or opportunities for progress, devising a strategic plan, and executing, and monitoring the introduced changes. The goal is to improve overall organizational performance and drive growth.

Job Analysis: a systematic process of gathering, documenting, and analyzing information about the work required for a job. This includes necessary skills, knowledge, tasks, and responsibilities necessary to perform the job effectively. It is crucial in ensuring correct hiring decisions, setting up appropriate compensation packages, performance appraisal measures, training needs assessment, and more. All these would eventually help the organization to achieve its business goals more efficiently.

Job Classification: A systematized process wherein jobs are categorized based on their duties, responsibilities, skills, knowledge requirements, and other job-related characteristics. This process is necessary to structure a fair and organized salary and benefits system within a company, maintain consistency in job evaluations and hiring decisions, and ensure compliance with labor laws and regulations.

Job Enrichment: The process of making a job more interesting, challenging, and satisfying for the employees.

Justice: The ethical principle that focuses on fairness, equality, and impartiality. It denotes the equal treatment of individuals without bias or favoritism, offering equal opportunities to everyone based on their abilities and performance. This principle ensures that every decision in the recruitment, compensation and management of employees is fair, transparent, and based on merit. Justice upholds the notion of "what is right" and maintains a harmonious, respectful, and productive workplace.

Knowledge Management: The process of creating, sharing, using, and managing the knowledge and information within an organization.

Knowledge Transfer: The systematic process of capturing, organizing, and disseminating information, skills, and competencies across teams and functions within an organization. The objective of this process is to enhance productivity, promote innovation, and encourage strategic growth. It may involve various methods such as mentoring, training programs, job shadowing, and utilizing knowledge management systems. Knowledge transfer is critical for preventing knowledge loss, encouraging continuous learning, and maintaining competitive advantage in the marketplace.

Leadership Development: The systematic process of empowering individuals with the skills, knowledge, and agility to effectively lead teams and organizations. This involves enhancing crucial leadership competencies such as strategic planning, decision-making, problem-solving, communication, team-building, and emotional intelligence. The goal is to ensure both current and future organizational leaders are prepared to navigate and drive business success amidst rapidly evolving business landscapes. Leadership

Development initiatives vary in structure and scope, encompassing coaching, workshops, cross-functional projects, formal degree programs, and more. Ultimately, they aim to foster a culture of continuous learning and are a key part of talent management strategies.

Learning and Development (L&D): A systematic process designed to improve the knowledge, skills, and abilities of employees. By focusing on employee learning and development, companies can help their employees stay competitive, adapt to, and implement new technologies, promote innovation, and foster organizational growth. This may involve a variety of activities such as training workshops, e-learning programs, leadership development programs, coaching and mentoring schemes. L&D programs need to be strategically structured to be in line with the company's goals and objectives to ensure long-term success.

Machine Learning (ML): An integral branch of artificial intelligence that leverages computer systems' ability to automatically learn and improve from experiences. Central to this process is empowering systems to access data, interpret it, learn from it, and subsequently make decisions with minimal human intervention. The focus is on enhancing the computers' accuracy and effectiveness in decision-making. ML's principal application spans predictive algorithms, data analytics, AI-powered automated processes, and trend analysis. ML, therefore, bridges computer programming, statistics, and predictive analysis, offering a robust tool for business optimization and intelligence.

Mentoring: A system of semi-structured guidance whereby one person shares their knowledge, skills, and experience to assist others' progression.

Merger and Acquisition (M&A): The consolidation of companies. A merger is when two companies combine to form a new entity, while an acquisition is when one company purchases another. These strategic moves are primarily made to create business growth, increase market share, decrease competition, or gain new technologies. The M&A process consists of three steps: pre-deal (including strategy and target search), deal execution (including due diligence and transaction), and post-deal (including integration). It is a complex procedure involving negotiations, finance, due diligence, and investment strategies.

Millennials: Also known as Generation Y, refer to the demographic cohort following Generation X. Born between 1981 and 1996, these individuals are typically characterized by their familiarity and engagement with digital technology, media, and communications. Compared to the previous generations, they are more likely to adopt and adapt to new technologies. In the workplace, millennials are known for their unique perspectives on employment and are often associated with a preference for a flat corporate culture and an emphasis on work-life balance.

Mission: A fundamental component of a company's strategic planning, providing direction and focus for all employees. It aims to inspire and motivate them, serving as a daily reminder of the purpose and direction of the company. It is also a statement to shareholders, customers, and the public of the company's intentions and values.

Moral Compass: The inherent ability of an individual to distinguish right from wrong and to behave accordingly. It is a guiding principle, shaped by personal values, beliefs, experiences, and societal norms, that influences our decisions and actions at the workplace. The integrity of an individual or an organization is largely dependent on the strength and direction of this moral compass. It serves as an internal benchmark, ensuring that our conduct remains ethical, fair, and consistent. Therefore, maintaining a strong moral compass is fundamental to creating a productive, respectful, and ethical working environment.

Natural Language Processing (NLP): The application of artificial intelligence (AI) to identify, understand, and respond to human language. It integrates computational linguistics with machine learning to cognize speech and text, enabling machines to mimic human understanding. NLP facilitates user interactions with digital systems like chatbots, virtual assistants, and search engines, enhancing their efficiency and accuracy. The technology also supports sentiment analysis, translation services, content summarization, and other advanced language processing tasks, playing a crucial role in automating, and optimizing business processes.

Negotiation Platforms: The structured environments, either physical or digital, where bargaining or negotiation processes take place. These platforms offer various tools that foster communication, collaboration, and decision-making between parties aiming to reach an agreement. Crucial features may include communication channels, document-sharing capacities, and mechanisms designed for proposals, counterproposals, or consensus building. The main goal of these platforms is to streamline the negotiation process and help all parties reach a mutually beneficial resolution.

Occupational Safety and Health Administration (OSHA): A regulatory body located in the United States. Its primary purpose is to ensure safe and healthy working conditions for working men and women by enforcing standards and providing training, outreach, education, and assistance.

Onboarding: The process of integrating a new employee into the organization and its culture.

On-The-Job Training (OJT): A hands-on method of teaching the skills, knowledge, and competencies needed for employees to perform a specific job within the workplace. Employees learn in an environment where they will need to practice the knowledge and skills obtained during training. This method puts the employee in an actual work setting and makes them a productive part of the team quickly. A key component of OJT is the on-the-job coach or trainer, who will provide guidance, instruction, and feedback to the employee. The goal of OJT is to increase productivity and efficiencies directly tied to the objectives of an organization.

Open-Door Policy: A communication policy in which senior management allows and encourages employees to approach them with any issue, feedback, or ideas they might have. This kind of policy fosters an environment of collaboration, trust, and mutual respect between the management and the employees.

Optimization: The process of making or adjusting a system, approach, or activity to make it as efficient, profitable, or effective as possible. This entails maximization of desired factors and minimization of undesired ones. In human resources, optimization can pertain to varying tasks, from streamlining recruitment processes for maximum efficiency to developing strategies to increase employee performance and productivity.

Organizational Restructuring: A substantial modification implemented in the overall organizational structure and processes of a company. It often involves altering authoritative lines, realigning responsibilities, and reallocating resources to better align with the firm's goals.

Reasons for restructuring can include cost reductions, succession planning, market shifts, a change of strategic direction, or improving competitiveness. The goal of restructuring is to enhance performance, and productivity, and align operations more closely to the business's vision. It is a significant process requiring careful planning and execution to ensure minimal disruption and a smooth transition.

Organizational Strategy: The actions and benchmarks a company set to achieve its long-term goals. It provides a blueprint on how a business will use its resources—such as labor, capital, and machinery—to cope with the competitive market environment.

Outsourcing: The business practice of contracting third-party service providers, domestically or internationally, to perform tasks or services that were initially conducted in-house. This approach often aims at cost reduction, productivity increase, focus on core competencies, or acquisition of specific skills not available internally. It covers a vast array of sectors like human resources, customer support, IT services, manufacturing, and more.

Parable: A brief narrative or allegory used to illustrate an instructive lesson or principle. It conveys its message indirectly by comparing or drawing a parallel with different situations or objects. Parables often have moral or spiritual lessons and are used extensively in philosophy, religious, and moral teachings.

Paradigm Shift: A fundamental change in the underlying concepts and experimental practices of a scientific discipline. It radically changes the underlying assumptions of a particular process, system, or industry. This shift can be brought upon by new ideologies, discoveries, or the evolution of market trends. It is significant as it steps away from the traditional conventions by replacing them with a new set of rules or frameworks, leading to improved effectiveness and efficiency.

Parity: The state of being equal, especially in terms of pay and opportunities. It encompasses a broad spectrum of employment practices, including equal pay for equal work, equal promotion opportunities, and equal access to training and development for all employees, regardless of their gender, ethnicity, age, or any other characteristic. Parity is a critical focus for organizations to ensure fairness, comply with laws and regulations, and optimize the use of their human capital.

Performance Management: The process through which managers ensure that employees' activities and outputs are congruent with the organization's goals.

Performance Metrics: These are quantifiable measures used to track and assess the quality and efficiency of services.

PESTEL Framework: An analytical tool for strategic business planning. It is an acronym for Political, Economic, Social, Technological, Environmental, and Legal factors, which are used to assess the market for a business or organizational unit. The framework helps organizations identify the various external factors that might affect their performance, thereby aiding them in planning and decision making.

Policy Formation: The process of creating, assessing, and implementing rules or regulations within an organization. In this procedure, the necessary actions to achieve specific goals are identified and codified into policies. These policies guide the decisions and actions of employees to ensure consistent and effective responses to various issues. Overall, policy formation is a crucial strategic activity that helps shape organizational behavior and drive desired outcomes.

Predictive Analytics: A category of data analytics aimed at making predictions about future outcomes based on historical data and analytics techniques such as statistical modeling and machine learning. This advanced form of analytics enables organizations to foresee future events and trends, thereby enhancing their decision-making capability and optimizing their strategic plans.

Problem Identification: A critical process that involves recognizing an existing issue or potential opportunity affecting the efficiency and effectiveness of the workforce.

Procurement: The strategic process of identifying, acquiring, and managing the goods and services that an organization requires to fulfill its business model. This includes activities such as sourcing suppliers, negotiating terms of contracts, and overseeing the quality and efficiency of the supplies obtained. It's a crucial function that aims to optimize operational efficiency, reduce risk, and drive value and savings for the organization.

Productivity: A measure of the proficiency of a system, frequently defined as the ratio of input to output within a particular time frame. It is generally calculated by dividing the total output by the total input, and the result demonstrates the total resources used in producing a particular quantity of output. By increasing productivity, businesses can realize greater profitability and operational effectiveness.

Protected Health Information (PHI): Any information about health status, provision of health care, or payment for health care that can be linked to a specific individual. This is interpreted rather broadly and includes any part of an individual's medical record or payment history. Under the U.S. Health Insurance Portability and Accountability Act (HIPAA), PHI that is linked to an individual includes 18 identifiers. If these identifiers are removed, the information is deemed de-identified and is not subject to HIPAA rules.

Public Scrutiny: Close examination and thorough inspection by the general public. This often involves a detailed analysis of an individual's or organization's actions, decisions, or products to ensure transparency, accountability, and to ascertain whether the best practices and ethical guidelines are being adhered to.

Public Sector HR Reformation: The process of modernizing and enhancing Human Resources practices within public sector entities. It involves initiatives aimed at improving recruitment, retention, performance management, and employee development. This reformation ensures more efficient use of resources, increased productivity, and improved service delivery. It's typically driven by forces such as technological advancements, budget constraints, changing workforce expectations, need for skill upgrading, and regulatory changes.

Quality of Work Life (QWL): The level of satisfaction, motivation, involvement, and commitment an individual experiences concerning their lives at work.

Rate of Absenteeism: The proportion of employees who habitually or frequently stay away from work. It is typically calculated as the ratio of the total number of workdays missed due to unauthorized or casual absences to the total number of workdays available during a certain period. This key performance indicator helps businesses identify potential issues related to employee engagement, job satisfaction, and company culture that need to be addressed.

Reasonable Accommodations: Modifications or adjustments to an application or hiring process, work environment, manner, or method of performing job tasks, or benefits and privileges of employment, that enable a qualified individual with a disability to perform essential job functions, enjoy equal benefits and privileges of employment as are enjoyed by similarly situated individuals without disabilities. These changes aim to facilitate equal opportunity, ensuring that workplaces are diverse, inclusive, and non-discriminatory.

Recruitment: The overall process of attracting, selecting, and appointing suitable candidates for jobs within an organization.

Religious Accommodation: The workplace refers to employers making certain adjustments or exceptions to standard workplace policies, practices, or routines, that would permit employees to practice or observe sincerely held religious beliefs or practices without undue hardship on the operation of the employer's business. Suitable accommodations can include flexible scheduling, voluntary shift swaps, job reassignments, or modifications of workplace policies or practices.

Remote Work: A flexible work arrangement that allows employees to work outside of a traditional office environment. It is based on the premise that work does not need to be done in a specific place in order to be executed successfully. Instead, individuals can perform their tasks and achieve their goals from any location. This working model leverages modern technology and digital communication tools to facilitate productivity and communication from diverse locations.

Resource Allocation: A crucial business process that involves assigning and managing assets, guidance, and duties within a company to maximize efficiency and productivity. It can range from human resources, financial assets, technological resources, and even time. Effective resource allocation guarantees that all different assets of an organization are employed efficiently, hence optimizing business performance.

Respect: An inherent acknowledgment and due consideration of the abilities, qualities, feelings, and distinctiveness of an individual or group. It involves treating others with courtesy, valuing their input and insights, and fostering an inclusive environment that appreciates diversity and promotes equal opportunities for all. A respectful workplace encourages open communication, collaboration, professional growth, and productivity. It's crucial that everyone adheres to the principle of respect, as it's a key element in maintaining a healthy and thriving work environment.

Retention: The ability of an organization to retain its employees. It is usually measured by the rate at which current employees choose to remain with the company rather than leaving or moving to a different organization. A crucial HR strategy that assists in maintaining continuity, reducing hiring costs, and ensuring organizational knowledge and experience remain within the company.

Risk Management: The process of identifying, assessing, and controlling threats or potential risks to an organization's capital and earnings. A strong Risk Management approach incorporates policies, technologies, and practices designed to mitigate risks and shelter the organization's resources and reputation.

Servant Leadership: A leadership approach that prioritizes the development and well-being of those being led. Followers are seen as important resources and emphasis is placed on their growth, engagement, and achievement. Servant leaders exemplify high levels of empathy, ethics, and focus on fostering a collaborative environment, enhancing the overall effectiveness and success of an organization. By making their team's needs a priority, they build a culture of trust and respect which ultimately pushes individual's performance and impacts bottom-line results.

Service Delivery Requirements: The specific expectations, standards, and metrics pertaining to the services that an organization offers to its clients or customers. These requirements are integral for ensuring that the service aligns with the company objectives and guarantees customer satisfaction. Service delivery requirements must be realistic, measurable, and agreed upon between both parties to ensure a smooth, efficient, and effective service delivery process.

Skill Gap: A phenomenon that occurs when employees' current abilities, proficiency, or knowledge do not meet the requisite demands or objectives of their job roles. In essence, when individuals lack the vital skills needed to perform their operations effectively and efficiently, a skill gap arises. Essentially, it signifies a development area where employees can enhance their current skills or attain new ones to reach their optimal performance level. Addressing skill gaps is critical to maintaining an engaged, competent workforce and achieving strategic business objectives.

Social Dynamics: The behavior, interactions, and changes that occur within social groups or between individuals in a social context. This concept encompasses a range of human interactions, social processes, and societal structures, including how these elements shape and are shaped by individuals' actions and mindsets. Understanding social dynamics is key to managing organizational culture and enhancing communication within a workplace setting.

Corporate Social Responsibility (CSR): A business model that helps companies be conscious of the kind of impact they are having on all aspects of society including economic, social, and environmental. It involves going beyond the legal requirements and obligations to pursue long-term goals that are beneficial for society. The core of social responsibility is ethical conduct, encompassing actions such as sustainable business practices, supporting nonprofit organizations, and implementing initiatives that benefit the community. This approach ensures a balance between economic growth and the welfare of society and the environment.

Social Welfare: A system that provides assistance and benefits, either directly or indirectly, to individuals or families in a society to ensure their well-being. This includes various programs designed to protect citizens from economic risks and insecurities, such as poverty, unemployment, medical costs, or other unforeseen financial difficulties. The primary objective is to enhance the quality of life, promote economic independence, and ensure a basic standard of living for all members of society.

Stakeholders: Any group or individual who has a vested interest in the success and decisions of a company. They can significantly influence or be influenced by the organization's operations, objectives, and policies. Key stakeholders typically include employees, customers, investors, suppliers, the community, and shareholders.

Stakeholder Management: A strategic approach used in business administration to attain mutual objectives and business goals. It involves identifying, analyzing, planning, and implementing actions toward stakeholders of a project or a business. It aids in understanding stakeholder perspectives, establishing communication, fostering cooperation, and addressing issues, ultimately leading to project success. Effective stakeholder management ensures two-way communication and cultivates durable relationships, resulting in a positive impact on business prosperity.

Stewardship: The responsibility of overseeing and protecting something valued, particularly an organization's assets. In a corporate context, stewardship is often linked with fiduciary duties to manage a company's resources efficiently, transparently, and in its stakeholders' best interests. It involves a commitment to serving the well-being of all stakeholders and safeguarding the company's sustainability and success over the long-term.

Strategic Decision-Making: The process of making choices or plans that are aimed at achieving long-term goals. These decisions involve a series of steps including identifying objectives, gathering, and analyzing data, generating alternatives, evaluating these alternatives, and monitoring the implementation and consequences of these decisions. This is conducted with a full understanding of the organization's internal capabilities and the external environment. Effective strategic decision-making allows businesses to take calculated risks, optimize resource allocation, align individual and departmental goals with the overall business objectives, and ultimately gain competitive advantage.

Strategic Human Resources Management (SHRM): A proactive approach to managing personnel. It aligns the human resources (HR) function with the strategic objectives of the organization. It enables the HR department to not just react to changes in the business environment, but to actively shape the workforce to meet the organization's goals. Tactics include developing talent, enhancing organizational culture, and improving employee engagement. SHRM helps the business to gain a competitive advantage by maximizing the effectiveness of its human capital.

Strategic Implementation: A crucial phase in strategic management where strategies and tactics are put into action to achieve organizational goals. It involves the design and execution of action plans to accomplish the strategy's objectives. This process requires comprehensive planning, employee engagement, resource allocation, and constant monitoring to ensure the strategy's success and alignment with the organization's mission and vision.

Strategic Networking: The deliberate process of developing and maintaining relationships, alliances, and connections to accrue knowledge, social capital, and further one's professional career or business interests. It includes identifying influencers, decision-makers, and individuals who can open doors to new opportunities. Strategic networking necessitates a proactive, focused, and purpose-driven approach to expand one's reach and influence within and outside one's industry.

Strategic Planning: A systematic approach to crafting long-term goals and translating them into achievable actions, allowing organizations to focus resources, synchronize team efforts, and align with core objectives.

Streamline: The process of enhancing efficiency in a company by eliminating non-value adding activities, reducing procedural redundancies or excess capacities. This is typically done through process automation, workforce training, rearranging certain operations or adopting new technology, with the end goal of saving time, reducing costs and improving overall efficiency.

Structured Data: A kind of data that is highly organized and formatted in a way that's easily discoverable by search engines. It's essentially data that is arranged in a predefined manner or model, such as a database, where it's managed using strict schemas. This type of data can be readily and seamlessly entered, stored, queried, and analyzed. Its key benefit lies in its efficiency and readiness for practical use in defined processes like data analysis or decision making.

Succession Planning: A strategic initiative that focuses on identifying and preparing suitable employees, through mentoring, training, and job rotation, to replace key leaders within an organization when they depart, retire, or are unable to perform their duties. This process ensures that businesses continue to operate efficiently without disruption during transitions. It also helps organizations prepare for all contingencies by developing high-potential workers for advancement into key roles. Thus, succession planning is essential for maintaining the stability and overall health of the organization.

SWOT: A strategic planning tool employed at the organizational level to evaluate the Strengths, Weaknesses, Opportunities, and Threats involved in achieving business objectives. Strengths and Weaknesses are internal factors under the control of the organization such as skills, resources, and assets. Opportunities and Threats are external factors beyond control such as market trends, competition, and economic environment. Combined, they provide valuable insights to form effective strategies and take calculated business decisions.

Symbiosis: A mutually beneficial relationship where two entities, often of different types, work together towards common objectives. This collaboration often results in increased productivity, efficiency, and value for both parties involved. It's a key concept in business, where collaboration between departments, companies, or individuals can drive innovation and progress.

Talent Management: A systematic process that organizations use to identify, recruit, retain, develop, and promote the most talented and superior employees available in the job market.

Talent Planning: A strategic approach utilized by organizations to meet their future staffing needs. This framework helps businesses align their human capital requirements with their long-term goals. It includes assessing current workforce skills and capacities, identifying potential gaps, and devising strategies to close these gaps.

Talent Pool: A database of potential candidates that a company maintains to meet its future human resource requirements. It consists of profiles of individuals who have been pre-assessed and identified as potentially suitable for certain roles within an organization. This proactive recruitment approach allows companies to effectively fill roles, reduce hiring costs and time, and ensure business continuity.

Teambuilding: A strategic process designed to foster a sense of unity, reinforce collaborative efforts, and nurture mutual respect within a group of individuals. It generally involves activities and exercises that require members to work together towards a common goal, thus driving productivity, enhancing communication, and improving problem-solving skills. Effective team building efforts can lead to increased efficiency, improved relationships, and higher overall employee satisfaction.

Technology Integration: The seamless incorporation of technology resources and technology-based practices into the daily routines, work, and management of organizations.

Termination Protocols: The standardized procedures followed when ending an employee's contract with an organization. Firstly, it involves clear communication of the reasons for termination, which could include performance issues, company downsizing, violation of company policies, or change in job requirements. Next, the employee should be given appropriate notice, as mandated by local labor laws, or as stipulated in the employment contract. This notice should be in writing and include the specific termination date. Any discussions or meetings regarding the termination should be conducted with sensitivity and respect, ideally in a private setting. It's usually preferable to have an HR representative present during such discussions. Further, ensure that all pending financial obligations, such as unpaid salary, bonuses, or benefits, are settled. Employees should also be guided on the transition of health care benefits, if applicable. Additionally, an exit interview, to gather feedback from the employee, should be conducted when feasible. Lastly, the retrieval of company property and access rights, and the transmission of relevant knowledge or job responsibilities should be managed in an orderly manner. It is crucial to document every step of the process and to maintain these records to safeguard against legal complications. Always consult with a legal advisor to ensure compliance with all relevant labor laws and regulations.

Total Reward Management: A holistic approach to employee rewards that encompasses various elements beyond traditional financial rewards or compensations. It includes aspects like career development opportunities, health and well-being benefits, recognition for contributions, a positive working environment, and work-life balance initiatives.

Transparency: The quality of a company being open, honest, and straightforward about its operations, decisions, and policies. The company must share relevant information with its stakeholders, which includes employees, investors, or the public.

Triple Bottom Line (TBL): A robust business framework that emphasizes three significant dimensions: social, environmental, and financial. Introduced by John Elkington in 1994, the approach aims at measuring the broader impact of an organization's activities on sustainability. The three dimensions also known as "people, planet, and profit", analyze an entity's social responsibility, its environmental impact, and its economic viability. TBL serves as a basis for companies to assess their performance in a broader perspective by including social and environmental factors besides the traditional financial metrics.

Turnover Rate: The percentage of employees that leave an organization during a certain time compared to the average number of employees. High turnover can be costly due to the time and resources spent on hiring and training new staff. It is a critical metric for organizations to monitor, as it can reflect the work environment and employee satisfaction levels.

Union (Labor): An organization of workers dedicated to protecting their interests and improving wages, hours, and working conditions.

Unstructured Data: Any data that is not categorized or structured for pre-defined data models or schemes. It typically includes formats like text files, videos, photos, email messages, social media posts, et cetera. A lack of structure can make comprehensive analysis more challenging, yet these kinds of data often hold a plethora of valuable insights.

Upward Communication: Allows lower levels in the hierarchy to provide feedback or make requests to higher levels.

U.S. Department of Labor (DOL): A federal agency that promotes the welfare and rights of American workers. Comprising of more than 25 sub-agencies, the DOL is primarily responsible for ensuring safe working conditions, administering benefits, and managing wage-related concerns. The DOL's responsibilities include the administration and enforcement of more than 180 federal laws and thousands of federal regulations that pertain to the U.S workforce. These regulations cover an expansive range of workplace activities, encompassing nearly all private, state, and local government employment across the United States.

Value: The tangible and intangible benefits that a company provides to its customers through its products or services. The value may include factors such as quality, price, convenience, customer service, brand reputation, and the overall customer experience. Delivering high value is crucial in standing out from the competition and achieving customer satisfaction and loyalty.

Vendor Management: The process that enables organizations to control costs, drive service excellence, and mitigate risks to gain increased value from their vendors. It involves activities such as selecting the right vendors, negotiating contracts, managing relationships, evaluating performance, and ensuring all commitments are met. Proper vendor management can result in long-term, mutually beneficial relationships between businesses and their vendors.

Virtues: The established desirable qualities or traits that are morally good and valued in an individual or organization. These may include professional attributes such as integrity, accountability, excellence, and respect among others. Virtues are the guiding principles that dictate behavior and actions, forming the basis for ethical business practices.

Vision Statement: A strategic guide for a company's decisions and goals, providing a clear, long-term direction. It serves as the company's roadmap, describing what the company wishes to achieve in the future and providing a clear criterion or set of standards for what the company is striving to achieve. This statement should be inspiring, enduring, and clear enough to guide both strategic planning and staff decision-making. Ideally, it reflects the organization's core ideology and ambitious goals, effectively motivating, guiding, and enlightening stakeholders about the company's intended course and purpose.

Visionary Leadership: A leadership style that encompasses the ability to create and articulate a realistic, credible, and attractive vision of the future that improves upon the present situation. It involves inspiring others to strive and achieve things they may not have imagined possible, driving strategic initiatives and transformation. Key traits of visionary leaders include strong strategic thinking, creativity, adaptability, persuasion, and empathy.

Voluntary Turnover: Voluntary termination of employees from the organization who leave by their choice.

Wage Garnishment: A legal procedure that allows a creditor to take a portion of an individual's earnings directly from their employer to repay a debt. This process typically commences after obtaining a court order. It's commonly used for debts such as unpaid child support, student loans, and credit card bills. This action is generally an action of last resort taken by creditors when other methods to recover the debt have failed. Employees need to be aware that federal law protects them by limiting the amount that can be garnished and prohibiting employers from terminating staff due to wage garnishment.

Wellness Programs: A type of proactive health initiative that employers offer to employees to promote and maintain their health and well-being. These programs typically include activities such as health education, weight management programs, medical screenings, on-site fitness programs, and more. The primary aim is to improve the overall health of employees, reduce healthcare costs, increase productivity, decrease absenteeism, and enhance employee morale.

Workforce: All the employees engaged in a particular organization, industry, or economy at a certain time. It consists of all the individuals performing tasks that contribute directly to the organizational goals. This covers both full-time and part-time employees, encompassing all levels of the hierarchy from entry-level employees to top executives. Understanding an organization's workforce is crucial for strategic planning, talent management, and ensuring labor law compliance.

Workforce Planning: The strategic alignment of an organization's human capital with its business direction. It involves analyzing the current workforce, determining future workforce needs, identifying the gap between the present and the future, and implementing solutions to close this gap. This systematic approach ensures optimal utilization of resources, decreases business risks, and improves decision making by predicting talent shortages and excess. Through effective workforce planning, organizations can better prepare for future staffing needs, eventually enhancing overall productivity.

Workforce Trends: Shifts in the labor market are often influenced by external factors such as demographic changes, economic conditions, technological advancements, and societal values. These trends can include changes in the composition of the workforce, employment rates, job types, work arrangements, employee expectations, and new skills required.

Recognizing and understanding these trends is crucial for optimizing human resource strategies and ensuring the long-term success of an organization.

Work-Life balance: The balance that an individual needs between time allocated for work and other aspects of life.

Workplace Culture: A system of shared assumptions, values, and beliefs, that govern how people behave in organizations. These shared values have a strong influence on the people in the organization and dictate how they dress, act, and perform their jobs. It manifests in various ways including leadership styles, communication patterns, and the degree of teamwork emphasized. Understanding workplace culture is essential for new hires to adapt quickly and for HR to develop strategies to encourage a conducive work environment.

Zero-hour contract: A type of contract where workers don't have guaranteed hours and agree to be potentially available for work as and when the employer requires it.

Author Bio

Aaron is a man molded by resilience, ambition, and determination. As a servant of Jesus Christ and fellow member of the Lumbee Tribe of North Carolina, Aaron's voyage from the humble beginnings in Prospect, North Carolina to the lush opportunities of the professional and academic world, is nothing short of inspiring.

In the meaningful lessons of Prospect Elementary School, Aaron discovered the precious value of community and unity. Roaring through the hallways and classrooms of Purnell Swett High School, he recognized the sense of self, the passion that each education stage was delicately crafting within him. He embraced this passion and allowed it to carve his path toward higher education and personal advancement.

At the University of North Carolina at Pembroke, Aaron dove head-first into the stimulating world of Criminal Justice, dedicating his years to understanding this field. He navigated through his discipline with admirable dedication, which ultimately led him to the gratifying day of his graduation where he was adorned with his hard-earned bachelor's degree.

Yet, the flame within him, the thirst for knowledge, refused to be quenched. This unending desire propelled Aaron to seek new horizons, guiding him to the culturally-rich city of Manchester, New Hampshire. There, at Southern New Hampshire University, he immersed himself in the Master of Science in Human Resources Management (MSc.HRM) followed by a Master of Business Administration (MBA). Aaron's remarkable journey paved the way for him to become a well-respected dignitary in his field.

But this academic laureate and HR professional never allowed complacency to hinder his growth. Aaron continued to challenge himself by stepping into the vortex of the corporate world, amassing in-depth experience at Fortune 500 companies. With each challenge, each hurdle, Aaron only saw opportunities for growth, wringing wisdom from every bit of his experiences.

Even while juggling the demands of his professional life, Aaron fueled his passion for learning by pursuing a Ph.D. in Public Administration at Liberty University. Every moment spent delving into the unchartered depths of knowledge is savored by this ardent learner.

Aaron's story is the epitome of relentless pursuit, passion, and determination. From Robeson County's quaint vibes to the professional playground of the corporate world, he has turned the pages of the vibrant book that is his life with zeal and anticipation. As a humble servant of Christ, an ambitious Lumbee, a scholar, an HR professional and a lifelong learner, Aaron serves as a beacon of inspiration for all who wish to turn life's chapters with unwavering determination. His journey elucidates one compelling truth: never stop learning, never stop growing, and never stop embracing life's boundless opportunities.